LET'S GO
TO THE
VIDEOTAPE!

LET'S GO TO THE VIDEOTAPE!

ALL THE PLAYS—AND REPLAYS— FROM MY LIFE IN SPORTS

WARNER WOLF

WITH LARRY WEISMAN

WARNER BOOKS

A Time Warner Company

Warner Books, Inc., 1271 Avenue of the Americas,
New York, NY 10020
Visit our Web site at www.warnerbooks.com

W A Time Warner Company

Printed in the United States of America
First Warner Books Printing: March 2000
10 9 8 7 6 5 4 3 2 1

Library of Congress Cataloging-in-Publication Data

Wolf, Warner.
    Let's go to the videotape! : all the plays—and replays—from my
life in sports / Warner Wolf with Larry Weisman.
      p. cm.
    Includes index.
    ISBN 0-446-52559-6
    1. Wolf, Warner. 2. Sportscasters—United States Biography.
3. Broadcasting Anecdotes. I. Weisman, Larry. II. Title.
GV742.42.W64A3 2000
070.4'49796'092—dc21
[B]   99-39614
                                             CIP

Book design by Giorgetta Bell McRee

This book is dedicated to my late parents, Jack and Rosemary Wolf, who taught me very early in life that nothing is impossible and provided me with all the love, confidence, direction and sense of humor that a young man could ever want. And also to the four women in my life—Sue, Joy, Shayna and Samantha.

Brief thanks to a few folks who had a hand in making this book a reality. To Don Imus, for suggesting I put my stories on paper. To Rick Wolff, my editor, for sifting and shaping a lifetime of memories. To Bob Castillo and Fred Chase, for their extraordinary eye for detail and for polishing this manuscript so that it shines; and to Dan Ambrosio, for serving as a most capable traffic cop in making certain the manuscript jumped over all the editorial hurdles. To Larry Weisman, who sharpened and focused the recollections and essays before your eyes. And to the many sports editors, producers and TV camerapeople who have tried to make me and my videotapes look good over the years.

Also, my sincere thanks to Roone Arledge, who brought me to New York in 1975 to advance my television career. And lastly, to the great sports fans in New York for listening to me over all these years.

CONTENTS

LET'S GO
TO THE
VIDEOTAPE!

1

MY MISSION STATEMENT

My philosophy on sportscasting isn't too complicated. In fact it's common sense. You have to be informative, you can't be silly, but you can be entertaining. I have always felt that television is an entertainment medium and sportscasting is part of that.

Face it. All the scores are the same. All the games are the same. Most of the stories on television are the same. The difference is how you present them.

I have always tried to find some kind of humor in the story. Now there's a thin line here. It has to be natural and it can't be offensive. You can't just make fun of somebody just for the sake of doing that. It can come out cruel. The key is to be clever when you throw in the good line. You can't be malicious or have a vendetta against someone. You aim to be light but to the point.

I picked this up from my parents. They were in vaudeville, show business folks, and we used to watch television and my

1

father, especially, could find something funny in any show, even if it wasn't a comedy. That's how I grew up—there was always a light side of it.

Also, growing up in Washington, I read two sportswriters every day, both of them gone now. That was Morrie Siegel and Shirley Povich. Both great. They were marvelous writers who could always find some bit of satire or a humorous side of any sporting event. I remember Povich writing about the 1948 Senators and he described them this way: They can't field, they can't pitch, but they can't hit either. He also had that great line about Jim Brown, back when the Redskins were the last team in the NFL without a black player. He mentioned how Jim Brown integrated their end zone a couple of times by scoring two touchdowns.

Plus the guys I hung around with all liked sports. We enjoyed it but didn't put life-or-death values on it. One day we're riding down Connecticut Avenue, and who comes out of a hotel? Bucky Harris, the Senators manager. So we yell to him, "Hey, Bucky, why didn't you bunt last night?" He just laughed, probably thought we were crazy kids.

Another time, after an expansion Senators game, standing outside of RKF Stadium, we saw Calvin Griffith, and this is after he moved the original Senators. We booed him, we razzed him, but it wasn't hateful.

That's where my philosophy comes from. I say what I think the fan is saying because I've been a fan and I'm still one today. If the New York Giants offense is horrible—and it is—I say, "You've heard of the prevent defense? The Giants are the only team in the league with a prevent offense." The fan relates to that. That's what he's saying.

Am I a journalist? Well, if your standard is Edward R. Murrow, no. If your standard is a person who communicates, yes, that's what I do and that's what I am—a communicator.

I am a writer. I've always written my own stuff on the air, every word I've ever said. When I started out, the longtime NBC sportscaster Jim Simpson gave me that advice when I was a young guy looking for a job. He said, "Always write your own stuff. People can tell when you're reading somebody else's work." I think that's the key to letting your personality come out on the air.

What I do, I take notes, I write them and rewrite them, I refer to them, but I don't use a TelePrompTer. People like to feel they're being spoken to, not read to or lectured. I used to watch Vince Bagli on the Baltimore stations and he always seemed as if he was talking to each individual viewer. I use that style—talk to people and make it humorous.

Why is that important? Well, I've always looked at sports and the weather as the comic relief on the newscast because usually the content of the news is so horrible.

But you can't force it. If you're not funny, don't try to be funny.

You have to be sure you never speak over the audience's head. Don't try to be smarter than they are. Keep it simple. Because you can turn an audience off very quickly if they think you are talking down to them or insulting their intelligence.

Now, I've always tried to find something funny every day in life, even under the worst circumstances. It comes naturally to me. I think I was the first guy really using the videotape to what it is today. And I was the first guy to fool around with names like ESPN's Chris Berman does now.

We had a weatherman, Frank Field. I'd say, "You remember his brother, Ebbets." There was a goalie named Trevor Kidd—I'd say, "Save by Kidd, no relation to Billy The."

My point is, if you're going to be successful in this business, if you're going to last, you have to be different from the other guy.

The other thing, and I've been very fortunate with this, is that people have to like you. They have to like you. I guess the only exception to that was Howard Cosell. A lot of people didn't like him but they watched him. A lot of people watched him because they hated him. But that's the exception. It's a lot easier if they like you. I've been very lucky in that New Yorkers made me feel very welcome both times here, the first time and when I came back. I owe a lot to the New York sports fans. They've provided me with a livelihood. They're very show-business-oriented so you can throw in these little bits and it doesn't go over their heads.

I've found it's important to take your work seriously, but not to take yourself seriously. You can razz a ballplayer but you have to know where to draw the line. This is how he makes his living. You have to have a little respect for what he does.

My style hasn't changed much. I guess this is my formula. This is what works for me. If you've got a shtick, you should shtick to your shtick.

2

LET'S GO TO THE VIDEOTAPE

Suppose we had videotape in the early twentieth century. You could go over the replays of the 1919 Black Sox World Series to help you decide if they really did throw games.

Did Joe Jackson, who hit .375 and made no errors, really take part in throwing the Series? You could look at all the errors. If they were taking a dive, why did the White Sox bother to win Games 6 and 7 of the best-of-nine Series? One answer could be that Dickie Kerr, who beat the Reds 5–4 in Game 6 (after beating them 3–0 in Game 3), was not involved in the fix. Or take Eddie Cicotte, a 29-game winner during the regular season who admitted before a grand jury a year later that he lobbed his pitches to the plate so slow in Game 1 (won by the Reds 9–1) that "you could read the trademark on the ball" and who committed two errors during the fifth inning of Game 4—he threw wild to first and then cut off a relay from Jackson in left that could have nailed a Cincinnati runner at the plate—that helped the Reds

5

score the two runs they would need to win, 2–0: He realized the players were not going to get the $100,000 from the gamblers as promised, so he went out in Game 7 and beat the Reds 4–1, going all the way on a 7-hitter. The next day Lefty Williams, a 23-game winner during the regular season but a loser in Game 2 (4–2) and Game 5 (5–0), gave up four runs in the first inning and the Reds went on to win the game 10–5 and the Series, 5 games to 3 (the Series had been extended that year to the best of nine, rather than the best of seven, for the extra revenue).

The thing that has always interested me about the scandal is that the following season, most of the White Sox players involved in the fix, knowing the scandal was still hanging over their heads (even though they had been acquitted by a Chicago jury in 1919), had great years. Cicotte, by this time thirty-six years old, won 21 games, while the twenty-seven-year-old Williams won 22. Jackson hit .382, knocked in 121 RBIs and led the league in triples, along with 42 doubles. Center fielder Oscar "Happy" Felsch, who had only heard about the conspiracy but didn't report it, hit .338 with 115 RBIs; George "Buck" Weaver, the third baseman, hit .333; and shortstop Charles "Swede" Risberg hit .266—a 23-point improvement over his lifetime average of .243. The remaining two of the "eight men out" were first baseman Arnold "Chick" Gandil and utility man Fred McMullin: Gandil, whom many historians believe was the player most responsible for the scandal—he spoke directly to the gamblers, maybe as much as a few weeks before the Series had even started—retired prior to the start of the 1920 season, at the age of thirty-one. McMullin played in only 46 games for the 1920 White Sox.

Or if there were videotape back then, you could go to the

6

1932 World Series and see if Babe Ruth really pointed to center field before hitting his famous "called" home run. There'd be interviews with him and the Cubs pitcher, Charlie Root, who later said, "If Ruth had pointed, I'd have knocked him down."

Or Dempsey–Tunney, where Gene Tunney was down 14 seconds. I know Tunney could have got up at the original count of 10, but would his head have been clear enough to stay away from Jack Dempsey the rest of the round?

Maybe that's why so many of these things are the stuff of legend. Nobody really knows. Word of mouth has a way of embellishing, and even the people who were there might not have had a really good look, and they tell other people what they thought they saw.

We're so used to the media being everywhere now that we're surprised when there is no videotape. The news seems incomplete without the moving pictures. And maybe that's why our legends don't seem quite so much larger than life. It isn't folklore anymore, folks. It's fact.

Not a problem today. Everybody's got the satellite, and highlights draw the viewers in. Remember when Howard Cosell used to mesmerize the audience on *Monday Night Football* with the halftime highlights from Sunday's games? Of course people were fascinated. For the most part this was their only shot at seeing all those games and all those plays boiled down into two or three minutes of fast action. With the technology today, they show the highlights practically as they happen, cutting into live broadcasts to show the plays from every game around the country. You don't need Monday night halftime highlights anymore. They're a day old. I saw 'em Sunday.

It wasn't quite as easy the first time I said "Let's go to the videotape." One night, I'm ready to show the tape of an NBA game, Lakers versus the Warriors. I say, "OK, let's look at Kareem Abdul-Jabbar going against Nate Thurmond last night."

Nothing comes up on the screen. No tape.

I say it again. "Let's look at Jabbar and Thurmond last night."

Still nothing. Just me, sitting there.

I yell to my director, Ernie Baur, who's with Fox in Washington now, "Hey, Ernie, the Jabbar tape."

Nothing. Now I'm hoping he's got this racked up and ready by now so I try one more time: "OK, let's go to the videotape."

And the tape rolled.

Boom. I've got a catchphrase. And it worked. The guys in the control room knew, when they heard that, to roll the tape. The audience knew they'd get to see the action. You can practically see everyone hunch forward when they hear those words, leaning in to get a look at what actually transpired.

You don't tell 'em in TV. You show 'em.

ON THE RADIO

April 1965. I was hired by WTOP radio in Washington. I'd been in radio for four years at this point, in Pikeville, Kentucky, and Martinsburg, West Virginia.

You know how I got my first job? I placed an ad in *Broadcasting* magazine, which now, in keeping with the times, is called *Broadcasting and Cable*. There was a space in the back of the magazine where you could put your own ad in the magazine. I got three responses—from Miami, Ohio, Terre Haute, Indiana, and Wilmington, North Carolina. The difference was that the guy from Pikeville called me up.

The interview on the phone consisted of two questions: Did I drink and was I ever in jail? I passed that test. I told him I had a couple of beers once in a while but I had never been in jail. So I got the job. Did everything, from sweeping the floors to playing the records and reading the news.

There was just one thing. I had to change my name to Ken Wolf. The general manager, Roy Alexander, said there was no one in Pikeville named Warner and it might be better if I picked another name. So for six months I was Ken Wolf.

Then I went to Martinsburg. And then Silver Spring, Maryland. And finally, I passed an audition at WTOP in Washington on the third try. Sam Donaldson worked there. Donaldson, of course, went on to become ABC's White House correspondent and is really one of the best journalists we've had—never hesitant to ask the probing question.

Here's my introduction to him. First day I'm in the newsroom, I ask if anybody's got a pencil. Donaldson throws one at me.

I guess that's how he got his point across.

4

NO BIG DEAL

It's April 1966. Seventh and final game of the NBA championship series, Lakers–Celtics, Boston Garden. I asked WTOP radio if I could go up to Boston by myself—hire a local Boston radio technician to plug us in and do the game myself, broadcasting it back to Washington. Believe it or not there was no national TV of the game, like there is now. Maybe some local broadcasts in a few cities but that was it.

Now, get this. Red Auerbach didn't even charge us to do the game. No rights fee. I did the play-by-play, the color, and kept score myself. The Celtics beat the Lakers 95–93, I packed up my stuff and I flew home the next day.

Need I tell you it's not quite that simple anymore?

5

MOE, LARRY, CURLY AND ME

One question I always get is if I'm related to the Three Stooges. Was Moe Howard my father, or Larry Fine, or even Curly or Shemp? And the answer is no. Emphatically no.

Here's how it got started. When the Three Stooges began, they were in vaudeville, just like my parents, Jack and Rosemary. The Stooges were managed by Ted Healy, who was also a comedian. He was a pretty funny man in his own right, did several movies. When the Three Stooges left vaudeville to go to Hollywood to make movies, Ted Healy had a hole in his act. He had all these bookings and he needed to fulfill these obligations.

Ted had seen my father perform with two other guys—one is a cousin, Mousie Garner, and the other was Dick Hakins. And unlike the Stooges, they were all musicians. And Ted approached them and asked if they'd like to replace the Stooges and help him continue his act while doing their own stuff. And they said yes. So that's where the association came from and you know what happens once a story gets started and told and twisted a little each time it's repeated.

There was a sportswriter at the old *Washington Star* named Russ White who once asked me about my parents and if I was related to the Stooges. After I explained the story, Russ seemed disappointed. He looked at me and said something only a sports guy would say: "So, your father was an expansion Stooge."

CAN'T GO HOME AGAIN

When I went back to Washington in 1992, I didn't exactly win any popularity contests and that was a big change from my first go-round in the 1960s and '70s. Things had changed.

My first time, at WTOP, we owned the market. There was Max Robinson and Gordon Peterson anchoring and Hilton Kaderli, who was a very popular weatherman. Nobody watched anything else. It was like the other two channels weren't even on. No contest. Max later went on to the ABC network and was highly successful before passing away in his early forties. Peterson is still the longest on-air anchorman in the country at the same station.

But when I came back, it was like starting all over. A lot of people who were watching now hadn't even been born when I started making my name in Washington, first in radio and later in TV. I was the new guy in town and certainly couldn't rely on my past laurels or reputation.

When you're the new guy, I've always felt, it takes at least three years for people to even know you're on the air. And now I was following a guy who had become a legend, Glenn Brenner, who had, with the exception of a few guys in between, replaced me after I left in 1976. Brenner was sharp, funny, he had a great rapport with Gordon Peterson and everyone loved him. Sadly, he died of a brain tumor in January of 1992 and was mourned literally by the entire town. Mourned and missed.

If you ever have a choice in life, you don't want to be the guy who follows a legend. You want to be the guy that follows the guy who immediately followed the legend. No matter how good or bad you are, you're never going to be as good as, in the fans' eye, the legend.

Another reason they say you can't go home again: If people do remember you from twenty-five years before, you may have become a myth in their heads. You may not have been as big or as good as they seem to remember but they talk about you. Then when you come back, they say, "What's the big deal?" It's like you're competing against your own legacy.

When I came back to Channel 9 in June of '92, the station was number one at five o'clock, number one at six o'clock and number two at eleven. When I left three years later, none of that had changed. Still number one at five, still number one at six, and number two at eleven. I made no impact either way in the three years. Not up, not down. However, the bottom line is that the termination by WUSA (formerly WTOP) turned out to be a blessing, giving me the opportunity to return to New York.

Off the Tube

From August to November of 1995 was the first time in thirty-five years that I was not on the air, radio or television. That's kind of a rude awakening. That's when you start thinking, "Oh, wow. Is this it? Is this the end?" You know the first person to call me the day after I was taken off the air? Dan Rather. I was sitting in my den and Rather calls and says there are only two kinds of people in our business: those who have been fired and those who will be.

Fortunately for me, in the fall of '95, I got a call from the Imus show. I'd known Don Imus since my New York days, first time around in '76. When Mike Breen couldn't do the I-man's show because he was on the road with the Knicks, they would call in guest sportscasters. I said, "Great." And apparently they liked the way I handled things for them because I've been doing it ever since as a sort of permanent substitute. Breen's away, I go in. By the way, let me say right now, going on the Imus show was a blessing. What a great place to mix humor and sports. Without question it is the most fun I have ever had on the air.

At the same time, the new sports talk radio show in Washington, WTEM, called. They'd been running Tony Kornheiser's show in the morning, taping it and playing it back in the afternoon but he didn't work on Thursdays. Same thing, they had guest sportscasters on Thursday and asked if I'd like to be one of the guests. I said, "Sure." And I guess they liked it enough that they made me the permanent fill-in on Thursdays for Kornheiser.

So from November of '95 through December of '96, that was my new title—permanent fill-in for Mike Breen and for Tony Kornheiser.

Then WCBS-TV in New York had a vacancy, called and asked me about coming back. And that was it. And it worked. It sure didn't hurt to have a presence in New York on the Imus show. And even when I wasn't on the show, Imus would promote me, telling the New York station general managers that they should bring me back to New York. There is no question that without Imus' input I would not have been asked to return to New York television.

But I also stayed ready for opportunity to present itself. You can't quit on yourself. You can't be unprepared. Now, one thing I did in that year and a half, I never stopped studying. I always read all the Washington and New York daily papers, plus *Sports Illustrated, The Sporting News, Ring* magazine, *Boxing Illustrated.* I stayed on top of the sports scene. I stayed active with it mentally, just in case.

A lot of folks equate their professional lives with their personal lives. One goes bad, the other goes bad. You can't let that happen. I knew TV could have its ups and downs. I'd had 'em before, though not like this. And the most important thing while being off the air became making sure I filled my time and didn't waste it on self-pity or brooding.

I mean, all of a sudden, here I am, fifty-seven years old, and except for filling in for Kornheiser on Thursday and flying to New York to fill in for Mike Breen, I've got all this spare time. You can't sit in your living room and stare at the four walls. And this wasn't about money or earning a living either, because WUSA-TV was still paying off the remaining twenty-two months of my contract, worth over a million dollars. Man, these guys must have really wanted to get rid of me, huh!

So I went around asking guys who were retired, "What do you do? How do you fill your time?" And they all said the same thing: "You have to have a purpose. You have to have another interest. You can't get up in the morning and have nothing planned. You have to have something to make you get up."

So I started filling in the days. Hmm. Well, Thursday's booked, working for WTEM. Same for the odd days on Imus. So what now? I looked to do things I had always wanted to do, things that got lost in the everyday pursuit of my career over the years. What kinds of things?

Teaching. I contacted George Washington University, Maryland and American University, told them about my availability and told them I could teach some sort of course in broadcasting. I felt that American showed the most interest and we worked out a program where they brought back a course called Sports Journalism they'd had years ago that was taught by Shirley Povich, the great writer from the *Washington Post*. It was a three-credit course on Wednesday nights from 5:30 to 8:00 and I'd have to say it was one of the most rewarding experiences I've ever had.

I had twenty-five students and interestingly enough twenty-four of them were from the New York–New Jersey area, so they had all grown up watching me on television. It was terrific. I taught them a lot of the history of sports, had them do their own sportscasts. I would try to show them the print, radio and TV versions of an event. We used a Grant-land Rice piece on the second Joe Louis–Max Schmeling fight from 1938. We'd have somebody read it aloud in class. We'd talk about how descriptive it was, and I'd ask, "Does it make you want to hear or see the fight? Well, here we go."

And then I played Clem McCarthy's radio account of the fight. And I said, "Now you've read it and heard it. Let's compare them." And then I said, "Now you're going to see it" and I showed them the film.

So the course went on for a semester and it was terrific. I feel like the students got a lot out of it and I know that I did. I only had to give one student a D. He just didn't show up. I should have failed him but I didn't have the heart.

One thing I did do in this class, on the very first day, was apply Vince Lombardi's principle—there's no such thing as late. The first day, students began walking in at 5:35 P.M., 5:40, 5:45, for the 5:30 class. I said, "NOT ACCEPTABLE." In this business there is no such thing as late. You're either there before the microphone or the camera or you're not. No such thing as late. From the next class until the end of the semester, no one was ever late. In fact, like the Packers in Lombardi's meetings, they showed up early—5:15, 5:20, 5:25. Unfortunately, I had no Super Bowl rings to give them.

In my game plan to take care of every day, I had now filled up Wednesday night and I had the WTEM show on Thursday. But I still had time and I still had plans. I had always thought French was a beautiful language, so for two months I took French from Berlitz. And the way Berlitz teaches, there's no English, it's all French, language immersion, just like when you were a baby and you learned to talk and read. So I learned a new language. But don't speak to me in French.

The problem is, if you don't have anyone to use the language on after you learn it, you forget it. I should have gone to work in a French restaurant. But I enjoyed the class, and my French wasn't bad.

Another thing I always wanted to do was fly. Always wanted to take flying lessons. I would drive by these little airports on the way to the beach in Ocean City, Maryland, or Rehoboth, Delaware, see those little planes and say, "I wish I could fly one of those." So I went out to this little airport in Gaithersburg, Maryland, and took flying lessons in a C-172 on Mondays.

It was wonderful, liberating. Once you got over any fear you had, it was terrific. I enjoyed the flying, the view from above, though I found that landing was the hardest thing. I had no problems taking off or flying the plane but landing was the toughest thing. The flight authorities go by hours and I had about twenty-five and reached the point where I was eligible to qualify for a license. But you know what? I was satisfied with what I could do and I never went back for the license. I realized I was never going to buy a plane. This was an accomplishment and I felt good that I could fly a plane. I flew with my daughter Shayna one time, flew out of Westchester Airport in White Plains, and it was really a thrill, though I think it took quite a bit of guts on her part. We flew over West Point and shared the joy of the landscape. It was beautiful.

So now I've filled up Monday, Tuesday, Wednesday and Thursday. One more day. I had started playing tennis when I was fifty, so I added a tennis game every Friday. Now my week was full, every day, and that was the way I passed the time. No sitting around. I thought it was great, terrific. I had reasons to get out of bed, things I wanted to do, plus my studying sports because I wasn't going to give up on the idea of being on the air again, and I was still getting paid from WUSA-TV.

And even though I had so many things to do, I couldn't picture myself retired. I'm sure there will come a day when they say I'm too old for television, but radio? If your voice is strong, you can be on forever. Paul Harvey is over eighty and he's still on every day.

All in all it was a great experience and a very interesting period. It taught me I have no interest in being retired. Work isn't work. Not working is a lot of work.

7

MEETING THE PRESIDENTS

Living in Washington over the years, I was fortunate enough to be invited to the White House on several occasions and had the privilege of meeting several of our Presidents.

I met President Nixon at the 1969 All-Star baseball game luncheon and made the protocol mistake of asking him for his autograph while on the greeting line. He was nice enough to oblige but frowned while signing.

I was invited by President Ford to a dinner honoring German chancellor Helmut Schmidt. Among those on hand were Joel Gray, Frank Langella and Rosalind Russell. As I passed through the reception line, President Ford introduced me as one of our leading sportscasters. That was a thrill. It was also neat to see the President and his wife, Betty, dance around the floor, just like any other couple.

In 1985 I met President Reagan at a Rose Garden White House ceremony put together by the National Sportscasters

Association. President Reagan spotted Vin Scully and said, "Just think. If I had stayed on as a sportscaster, I might be doing the Dodgers games today and Vin Scully might be President." That got a good laugh. Ronald Reagan, back in the '30s, did studio re-creations of Chicago Cubs games in Des Moines, Iowa.

Then came a moment when I found myself in the corner of the East Room with the President—just the two of us. Being such a great movie fan, all I could think of was that *Desperate Journey,* made in 1942, would be shown that night on satellite TV. So I said, "Mr. President, do you know what's on TV tonight?" And Mr. Reagan said no. And I said, "*Desperate Journey,* with you and Errol Flynn."

He pauses, looks at me and says, "*Desperate Journey, Desperate Journey.* Wow, that was a long time ago!" And he walks away.

Later, here's all I could think of: The President of the United States, one of the busiest and most important men in the world, is probably thinking about how to keep the peace, how to balance the budget, and here's a guy asking him about *Desperate Journey.*

He probably thought I was on a desperate journey.

8

DON'T LOOK NOW

In 1990, I was asked to be the MC of a charity boxing luncheon at the Plaza Hotel, with the proceeds from this function going to benefit a Queens Boys Club.

For me it was great! I got to introduce Muhammad Ali, Joe Frazier, Jersey Joe Walcott, George Foreman and Larry Holmes—five heavyweight champions, all on one dais.

Well, any time you're an MC, and especially at a luncheon, where people have to get in and get out and go back to work, you always want to be upbeat and keep the program moving. When you have guys like Ali, Frazier, Foreman, Holmes and Walcott, it should be easy. These guys are stars, celebrities, and people want to see 'em.

So I'm sitting at the dais going over my notes, really getting up for the luncheon, when who walks in with an entourage, surrounded by bodyguards? New York crime boss John Gotti, the famed Dapper Don.

The chairman of the luncheon, before turning the microphone over to me, introduces people from the audience and says, "And we want to especially thank John Gotti for buying a table and tickets for the benefit of the Queens Boys Club."

As I got up and introduced each fighter, I noticed (and this was a first when speaking before a group) that I totally blocked off one side of the room. I wanted to make sure that I did not stare at Gotti or his table. As a result, I overcompensated and never looked at the left side of the room. I looked straight ahead or to the right.

I did not want to make any eye contact. I didn't want to be put in the position where I might be asked to come over to his table after the luncheon. Maybe it's because it reminded me of a story my father told me that had occurred fifty-eight years before in Chicago, in 1932, during Prohibition.

Remember I told you about my father being a replacement Stooge in vaudeville? Well, he and the other two substitute Stooges—Mousie Garner and Dick Hakins—had just performed at the Apollo Theatre in Chicago, with Al Capone and his men sitting in the front row.

After the show, the Stooges' manager, Ted Healy, told my father that Capone enjoyed the show so much that he wanted my father and the other two Stooges to personally perform for him and his friends at his private club.

My father and the other two Stooges said, "Gee, we're tired. We've just done three shows." And Healy said, "Look, I don't care how many shows you've done and how tired you are. When Capone says he wants to see you at his club, he's not really asking. You just go."

According to my father, this became an offer he couldn't refuse. So they went. When they arrived, Capone personally shook their hands. They did the show and left. And no, there was no overtime pay.

9

PROPHETIC WORDS

As I mentioned earlier, when WUSA in Washington fired me, I got paid for over a year and a half. There was a little irony in those pay envelopes too. That was exactly the situation I had used on the air for years when a coach would get fired with time remaining on his contract.

I would say, for example, "The Redskins fired Richie Petitbon today. They will now pay Petitbon $500,000 a year for the next two years not to coach the Skins."

This time the joke was on me. What happened to all those coaches happened to me. WUSA will now pay Warner Wolf over a million dollars over the next twenty-two months not to do the sports on WUSA. It was poetic justice.

THE IMUS SHOW

One of the first questions most people ask me nowadays is about working on the *Imus in the Morning* radio show. People are very curious about Imus, want to know what he's really like, because he doesn't always come across as someone you'd want to sit next to in your carpool.

First of all, let me tell you that Don Imus is a very loyal, good-hearted, generous person. And I'm not just sucking up to him, as he would say.

Sure, he sounds cranky most of the time but you just have to understand him and the way he approaches the show. I'm not saying he won't go after you if you say something to get on the wrong side of him or you mess up on the show. But if you do your job, contribute to the program and hopefully bring some humor to the table, you're gonna be OK.

The thing you want to remember is this: If Imus goes into a tirade on the show, really lambasting someone or something someone has done, that doesn't necessarily mean that he hates that person. It means that that person or that particular issue (usually topical, timely and fair game on that specific day) provides great radio material for Imus to get a controversial bit going. He may not hate that person or even dislike him. In fact, he might even like the person. It doesn't matter. Everyone is fair game.

The point is, by using his technique, he is involving you in the thought process and the discussion. He's bringing you into the picture—whether you're at home and getting ready for work or whether you're already in your car. You're interested in what he's saying. There's passion there. It's not important that you agree or disagree, the bottom line is that your mind is taking part in the discussion. It's his job to keep you hooked.

And he's got to keep it going from 5:30 A.M. to 10:00 A.M., five days a week. He has to be prepared enough that you will want to tune in and stay tuned for all or some part of those four and a half hours. I'll tell you this, the man's prepared! He reads more books and newspaper editorials and watches more news-related programs than any on-the-air person I know. I don't know where he gets the time and when he sleeps (though he looks like he doesn't sleep that much). Heck, he's in his office by 5:00 A.M. He's already there when I arrive at 5:15.

I wish you could see his office. It's really a warm, dark, comfortable room. He has thousands of books stuffed into his bookshelves and a huge jukebox. The lighting is low. It would be easy to doze off in Imus' office, but who would risk that and be caught by Imus?

It's hard to get anything by him. The lineup of guests he has each week is like a who's-who or Hall of Fame, from all fields. The people want to be on his show. Number one, they know they'll be heard by millions of listeners. Number two, besides being given a chance to say what they want to say, they know that Imus will bring out a human side, and often a humorous side, of them that might not be heard anywhere else.

Now before I tell you about my experiences with the I-man, let me say Imus is very fortunate to have with him Charles McCord, who doubles as his newsman. He's very good at it, did it for years as a straight news guy. I don't know anyone who could play off Imus the way he does. To be clever and supporting but at the same time calling Imus right down on the spot, on a statement that could be deemed outrageous. The rapport between the two of them sort of keeps an invisible boundary around the show.

Then there is Bernard McGuirk. Very quick mind. Bernard, who does a lot of voices, along with Larry Kinney and Rob Bartlett, is the voice of Cardinal O'Connor. He jumps right in, never missing an opportunity to add to the levity. The key with Bernard is his timing. He never steps on the I-man or McCord. He strikes at the right time. He is the king of satire and the timely razz.

Bernard is also an outstanding impersonator of various ethnic types. You'd be surprised how many people think Nets forward Jayson Williams just called in when it was really Bernard. I actually thought it was Jayson until I was told it was Bernard.

Rounding out the crew is Lou Ruffino, Imus' longtime engineer. You'll hear Lou's voice pop in and out during the bits. Like when I'll say, "Say so long to Dennis Rodman, who's been released by the Lakers," and Lou starts going "So long, so long, get him out."

I've always said Imus brought me back from the dead. As

you know, I had been taken off the air in August of 1995 by WUSA-TV in Washington. Then I received a call from Mark Chernoff, the program director of WFAN in New York, in November of '95, asking me if I would appear for a day as a substitute sportscaster on the Imus show. As I mentioned, Mike Breen, the regular sports guy and a play-by-play man, had another assignment. Chernoff said Imus recommended we get Warner Wolf to do the show.

Well, I flew up, did the show, and was invited back a few weeks later and have been doing the show, substituting for Breen, ever since.

First of all, you write and read your own stuff (like I do on television) but you have a little more leeway here with the writing. You can say things on radio that you can't say on TV. Secondly, and most important, you have guys playing off you and responding to you. You don't have that on TV. And the other thing is, you don't have to get dressed up. No tie. Jeans and shirt or sweater or jacket if you want. Very relaxed. Don't forget, I was in radio eight years before I did TV and then did both, radio and TV, at WTOP in Washington, for eleven more years. So I am no stranger to radio.

The ironic thing is, when I was doing the sports call-in show on WTOP radio in 1965, my newsman was none other than Charles McCord. And here we are, over thirty years later, working on the same show.

So how did Imus revive my career and help bring me back to New York? In the almost year and a half I was off TV, every time I flew up to New York and appeared on his show, Imus would be like a personal public relations man, telling the New York TV stations to bring me back and put me on the air. It was great. It was like he was my campaign manager.

Sure enough, with the help of Imus' constant calls for my return and my appearances on his show, I got a call from Bud Carey, then the general manager at WCBS-TV. I was hired and went back on the air at Channel 2 February 3, 1997.

If he never did another thing for me he would have done enough but in July of 1998, during an appearance on his show, Imus says to me, "Why don't you write a book?"

Well, I told him I did, in 1983, called *Gimme a Break*. It was published by McGraw-Hill (and then Avon paperbacks in 1984). And he says, "Well, that was fifteen years ago. Why don't you write another one?"

Believe it or not, one day later, the phone rings at WCBS and it's Rick Wolff, a senior editor at Warner Books. He says he just heard the Imus show and would I be interested in writing another book? Well, the rest is history. The book you are reading was born on that broadcast. So I do feel indebted to Imus.

Which doesn't mean I won't try to sneak one past him. Breen and I always try to do that. It's like playing a trick on your uncle. For example, in December of 1996, Rex Chapman and the Phoenix Suns lost a triple-overtime game to Detroit in which the Suns scored only six points in the third overtime. Just before the 6:40 A.M. sports, I went next door into the production room with producer Craig Chamides (a very helpful and talented individual) and recorded a ten-second sound bite, pretending to be Rex Chapman.

Keep in mind that Imus is very busy at this time, doing the show. He usually can't see you in the production studio. So we go on the air and I say, "Detroit and Phoenix went into triple overtime last night. Phoenix lost the game. Rex Chapman was asked about the loss."

Usually you get the standard response about a tough defeat but the sound bite we prepared had Chapman saying: "Who cares? We don't get paid overtime."

As I started to move on to the next story, Imus looks up and says, "Hey, wait a minute. That wasn't Rex Chapman. I thought I told you to stay out of the production room. Put a lock on that door."

And then Bernard says, "You can't get one by the I-man."

The day before Thanksgiving in 1998, I said, "The Vikings play the Cowboys and the Steelers go against the Lions. Charlie Batch will quarterback the Lions, replacing Bobby Layne."

As I'm going on to the next story, Imus says, "Hey, wait a minute. You think I wasn't paying attention? Bobby Layne? Come on. Do you think I'm that senile? Is that what you think, that I'm totally senile? You and Breen are trying to get away with that stuff."

Breen, by the way, is very funny, the master of the interchanging sound bite, using an old voice of somebody else, rather than the actual player, to describe something. It's all a part of the whole atmosphere Imus creates. Nothing is sacred, everything is in play. He'll get off on a tangent and keep pursuing it until it plays itself out.

In June of '98, my wife and I had gone to the French Open. So Imus says to me on the show, "Did you take the Concorde?" I said no. "First class?" No! "Business class?" No! "What? You flew coach?" Yes. "You're an embarrassment to the show."

And he kept on. "How did you get to the matches from the hotel? Limo?" No. "Rent a car?" No. "Taxi?" No. "How did you go?" The tour bus, I told him. "You took the

tour bus? With a lot of fat tourists? You are an embarrassment. Get off the show."

Now that was funny. He made a great bit out of an innocent situation, out of something ordinary and everyday.
That's what makes him so good.

Sometimes Imus allows me to stay in the studio with
Charles McCord after the sportscast and join in with the
next guest. On one occasion, Pat O'Brien, co-host of *Access
Hollywood,* called in. It was around Christmas. Pat had
written a little ditty to the tune "The Twelve Days of Christmas," with each day involving Imus.

Talk about dragging on. After the fifth day, Imus butts in
and says, "This bit is going nowhere. That's it, Pat. You're
off. Man, that was lame."

So I said, "You know it. It's one thing to be long, but when
you're long and BAD, that's worse." Everybody laughed. But
the point is, Imus loves Pat O'Brien. He's a good friend of his
and would do nothing to hurt him. But here was an opportunity to poke fun and make good radio and that is the bottom line for Imus. That is what his show is all about.

The first time I ever met Imus, his attorney, Mike Lynn,
who was a neighbor of mine, took my wife and me to a club
where Imus was appearing. Imus is also a great standup comedian, and that's where he gets his timing from. I've seen
him MC luncheons and he is hilarious. Great at satire and
capturing the mood of the audience, very contemporary.

When he made that now-famous speech at the Radio and
TV Correspondents Dinner in Washington in front of President Clinton and Hillary, he got a lot of flak. The thing that
struck me about it was that Imus was making a joke about
the President fooling around long before the Paula Jones and
Monica Lewinsky scandals came out. President Clinton,

who had been laughing at the material up to that point, suddenly turned to Imus and gave him one of the nastiest looks of all time.

Well, as we look back on that glare now, that was a dead giveaway. Imus had obviously hit a sore spot. An innocent man would have had nothing to hide and would have laughed it off. Why would he care about a joke on him if it wasn't true? But by reacting that way, President Clinton tipped his hand. Only a guilty man would have been that upset.

It's not like Imus hasn't climbed all over me too. You have to expect it. During the year and a half when I was off TV and in one of my fill-in performances for Breen, my sportscast seemed to go on a little too long. Included was my complaint that most baseball managers don't let their starting pitchers throw complete games. They baby the pitchers and take 'em out after five or six innings, even though they're pitching strong games. Well, I went on and on, maybe belaboring the issue.

Finally, Imus looks at me and says, "Warner, nobody cares. This is why you're not on TV anymore." Now that makes for a funny radio moment. He shoots you down in mid-flight. Once Imus got up out of his chair, went into his briefcase, pulled out a .357 Magnum and threatened to shoot me because my sportscast was too long. But I know he's only kidding.

At least I think he's only kidding.

11

THE FUTURE IS NOW

One expression I've used over the years on the Imus show is "The future is now." I just plain stole this one from George Allen, whom I got to know when he coached the Redskins.

Nice, tidy phrase. Sums it all up. Tomorrow is only a promise. Today is here, right now.

That was the way George answered the questions about trading draft picks for older veteran players. Someone would ask, "How can you sacrifice the future?" And George would respond, "The future is now."

He proved to be right, because he took the Redskins, who had won nothing for years, to the playoffs and then the Super Bowl.

Well, about three years ago, I'm on the Imus show one morning and I'm reporting on a hockey trade. The team had swapped three prospects for one aging veteran. I said to

Imus, "Do you know why they made that trade? Because the future is now."

And Imus, Charles McCord, Bernard and Lou all jumped in: "Yeah, the future is now."

And it is. Not tomorrow, not two weeks from now, the future is now. More and more, people want results and they want them now. Don't tell me about the kid who's going to be a star, because maybe he won't be. And don't ask me to wait for you to win that championship because that's the same as dreaming. If there's one piece missing from the puzzle, go get it and solve tomorrow's problems later.

So any time a young guy is traded for an old guy in any sport, you can bet on the Imus show that you will definitely hear "The future is now."

Somewhere, I know George Allen is smiling.

12

NO MATINEES

My father, in trying to impress upon me the necessity of giving it your best at all times, used to have this expression: There are no matinees. In other words, just because you may think that, for whatever reason, no one is watching, you can't lay down. You still have to give it your best shot every time.

That old saying came from his vaudeville days. It seems that many times, during the weekday matinee in the late '20s and early '30s, a lot of the big headliners would take off and call in sick—because the matinee usually drew less than the evening or weekend show.

Well, many years later on the Imus show, I thought about my father's advice.

Every year the Imus show is broadcast from the World Financial Center, live from 5:30 A.M. to 10:00 A.M., to raise money for the C.J. Foundation. In 1999, in fact, the show raised over $2.5 million in forty-eight hours, so you know what kind of reach the I-man has. On this particular morning in February of 1999, the first sportscast of the day was scheduled for 5:40 A.M. My initial thought was to go easy at that hour. That's certainly not the peak listening time and there were four more shows to do, so why not save some of the material?

You know what? Imus gave me a lead-in and I just took off. Playing off Imus, I might have produced the most humorous, enthusiastic sportscast I ever did. It didn't matter that there might have been a smaller listening audience and that there were only about ten people sitting in at the moment at the World Financial Center. He fed me and we just took off and it was great! And guess what?

Because Imus interviews people on this program to help with the fund-raising, I did not do four more shows that day. I only did one. Now suppose I had tried to just slide or ease by in that first segment at 5:40, thinking about how I would dazzle everybody later? Well, I know I would have been upset with myself for saving some of my lines. It would have bothered me for a long time, since I only did one more sportscast.

My father was right. There are no matinees. And you are only as good as your last show.

BROTHERLY LOVE

One final word about Imus. Besides his wife and son, from what I can see, Imus really loves his brother Fred. While most brothers may not be that close, Imus genuinely loves Fred.

You'll notice as Imus says goodbye to Fred on the air, he'll end it with, "I love you" and Fred says, "I love you."

Never having had a brother—or sister, for that matter—it's nice to see adult siblings still maintaining close family ties.

14

EARLY RISER

People constantly ask me, "How can you do the late-night news on CBS-TV and then get up at 4:30 A.M. and do the Imus show?"

Well, the answer is—it's fun. As I said, it is the most fun I've ever had in my thirty-nine years on the air.

As far as getting up at 4:30 A.M. after doing the late sports until 11:30 P.M. and getting to bed by 12:30 A.M.? The key is: NO BOOZE, going straight home and going right to bed. If you start hanging out after the late sportscast and/or boozing it up, you're going to have a tough time.

GIVE ME A BREAK

Most of the expressions you heard in the late '60s don't come up in conversation anymore. When is the last time you heard someone say, "Cool, man! That's neat." Has anyone told you something was groovy or far-out lately? Nope. Now it's "Hey, dude" or "chill."

But besides "Let's go to the videotape" and "BOOM!" and "Swish!", another phrase which has stuck around is "Come on, give us a break" or the simple, plaintive, "Gimme a break!"

I started using that phrase in 1968. The Redskins played the Lions the last game of the season and won the game 14–3. However, the Skins appeared to get a really bad call in that game. I showed the play the next day on my TV show and said, "Come on, ref. Give us a break." Everyone on the set laughed and said, "Yeah, come on, give us a break."

It is the cry of the underdog, or the man who has been shortchanged. And I never stopped using it.

It was also the title of my first book. Funny thing. The TV show called *Gimme a Break!*, which came along about twelve years after I first used the expression, tried to sue us to prevent the book from coming out. We told them to buzz off and if anybody was stealing the phrase, it was them.

They dropped the suit. They gave us a break!

16

THE PRICE OF FAME

I'm on jury duty one time, criminal case, Manhattan. Comes 7:00 P.M., the judge says, "We want to reach a verdict but by law we have to feed you and then you come back. We're going to have to take you to a restaurant as a group. The police will escort you but you can't talk to anybody. It's called being sequestered."

So they take us to a restaurant where you have to walk through the bar in front to get to the dining room. As I'm sitting in the back with my fellow jurors, with two armed guards watching us, a guy who's a little boozed from the bar walks over to my table with a pen and a paper and says, "Warner, can I have an autograph?"

Now because we were sequestered and not allowed to talk to anyone, the guards jumped up and grabbed this guy, escorted him right out of the bar. And he's saying, "I only wanted his autograph. I only wanted his autograph."

And all I can think is, to this day this guy probably figures Warner Wolf travels around with armed bodyguards.

HANDS OF STONE

George Plimpton made a name for himself by playing with some pro sports teams and writing about the difficulties he encountered. You remember *Paper Lion,* where he suited up at quarterback for the Detroit Lions. Well, it doesn't always work out so well.

In May of 1973, the Redskins were holding a minicamp at Redskin Park and I had an idea for a story. I called the Redskins and asked if I could come out, bring a camera crew, and shoot Billy Kilmer throwing passes to me. You know, what's it like to catch a pass thrown by an NFL quarterback? He would tell me what route to run and I would run the pattern.

No problem, the Skins say. Billy would be happy to do it. So I show up there, ready to roll. I go out for a few passes and I don't catch one, either running the wrong route or dropping the ball.

Finally, Kilmer says, "Look, line up wide, go ten yards downfield, cut across the middle and the ball will be there."

Well, I did and it was. My first and only catch. The one minor problem was that he threw the ball so hard he cracked a bone in my right thumb. I never realized how hard a professional quarterback throws the ball. I looked up and boom! Right in my hands, but my thumb got in the way.

I didn't want him to know he hurt me so I thanked him for taking part in the story and left—without shaking hands with my right hand.

Some people said Kilmer didn't have a great arm. You couldn't prove it by me.

WARNER THE JOCK

My best sport was softball. I always played center field from the time I was about twelve years old until I stopped playing when I was in my forties. I was a good outfielder but I couldn't hit. I could always get a jump on the ball and usually run it down.

At George Washington University, we had intramural teams primarily made up of fraternities and my fraternity had so many great softball players we actually had A and B teams. I was on the B team and it was so strong that both the A and B teams made it to the semifinals of the entire university. Of the final four, Phi Alpha had two entries.

One game, we played against the GW football team's softball team. There was a guy named Moose who was an offensive tackle and he actually hit a ball that had to go 350 feet. That's a long shot for a softball. I can just remember running and running—we played on the Ellipse outside the White House and there aren't any fences—and I'm running and running and I reached out over my shoulder and caught the ball. Best catch I ever made. We won the game 8–4.

My father used to come down and watch the games. He was the only one there. He used to bring a little portable seat and set it up and watch. One time, fly ball to right center, I let the ball drop. Bad communication between me and the right fielder, Richie Pincus. And I threw my glove on the ground. And my father stopped the game and ran out on the field.

Here I am in college, twenty years old, and there's my father telling me, "I never want to see you do that again. That's bad sportsmanship." And then he turned around and walked off the field. I was embarrassed, but he was right.

Another time, I came up with the bases loaded and my father got out of his chair and called time-out. He's not even a member of the team and he's calling time-out! He comes up to me outside the batter's box and tells me to change my stance and place my left foot toward the pitcher. I hit a ball right up the middle for a two-run single and we won the game 3–2. I always thought my father could have been a good coach.

Played a lot of softball. Enjoyed it. I knew I'd had it when, after all these years, I couldn't cover the ground anymore and had to start playing right field. I was working for WABC-TV, we're playing a game and I'm in right field. Geraldo Rivera hits a long drive to right—not as long as Moose's ball—and I went back and caught the ball and broke my finger.

That was it. I figured if I can't catch a fly ball anymore without breaking anything, I'm done. I came in, stuck my finger in the ice tub with all the beers and called it a career.

I did break my ankle once playing intramurals at GW in the only game I wore spikes. Never wore 'em again.

Used to play touch football every Sunday in Washington. In 1972, Sonny Jurgensen had snapped his Achilles tendon when he stepped in a hole playing the Giants at Yankee Stadium. No one even knew what an Achilles tendon was until Sonny hurt his. Three weeks later, I'm playing touch football at Churchill High School's field, it's a cold day, I'm running down the field and I thought somebody kicked me in the back of the heel from behind. I turn around, there's nobody there.

I ruptured my Achilles tendon. Sonny and me. No one had ever heard of an Achilles tendon before and now this. They put Sonny and me in a commercial together. Just tendon to business, I guess.

19

I'M ENSHRINED

Two of the great thrills I have had over the years as a sportscaster were inductions—into the New York and the Greater Washington, D.C., Jewish Sports Halls of Fame.

In 1993 I was selected for the Washington Hall of Fame, located in nearby Rockville, Maryland. I was inducted with two of my heroes, Red Auerbach, who still lives in Washington, and *Washington Post* sportswriter Shirley Povich.

In 1999 I was inducted into the New York Jewish Sports Hall of Fame, located in Suffolk County, on Long Island. I went in with Kenny Holtzman—who won 174 games in a fifteen-year career with the Cubs, Orioles, A's and Yanks— and the late, great boxing trainer and manager Ray Arcel.

For my money, Auerbach had the greatest basketball mind as a coach and general manager in the history of the game. Perhaps no one will ever beat his Celtics coaching record of eight consecutive NBA championships and nine out of ten. And who was better than Auerbach as a trader? Getting

Robert Parish from the Warriors for two draft picks, obtaining Bill Russell for Easy Ed McCauley and Cliff Hagan in 1956, having the foresight to draft Larry Bird a year before he could even play in the NBA. He also talked Danny Ainge out of a baseball career with the Toronto Blue Jays as an infielder to play for Boston.

And in New York, what an honor to be inducted with Ray Arcel. A real legend in the ring, who managed and trained more different champions than any other trainer in boxing history.

Arcel trained twelve fighters who fought Joe Louis—and all twelve lost. Arcel told me that all twelve were afraid of Louis before they even entered the ring and there was no chance they were going to win. He was also the trainer of Roberto Duran when he did his "no mas" fight against Sugar Ray Leonard in 1981 and quit in the ring. Arcel later told me that in his more than seventy years in the ring, it was the first and only time (barring an injury) that he ever saw a man just suddenly stop and quit in the ring.

Apparently, boxing officials got together after the fight that night to question Duran and consider holding up his purse for this fight. Arcel got a call at one o'clock in the morning telling him Duran was going to face the committee. Arcel got out of bed and went down to be with Duran.

Before leaving his hotel room, Arcel was asked why he would go out at one o'clock in the morning to try and help a fighter who just quit on him and everyone else. Said the eighty-year-old Arcel: "He's still my fighter and it's my responsibility to help him if I can."

How's that for loyalty?

A LIVING LINCOLN MEMORIAL

As far as I know, I am the only living Jewish relative of Abraham Lincoln.

No, Lincoln wasn't Jewish. Let me explain and tell you a little about my family.

My maternal grandmother was Lyla Hanks, a journalist and newspaper editor from Springfield, Illinois. Lyla Hanks was a cousin of Nancy Hanks, Lincoln's mother. When my mother married my father in 1933 she converted to Judaism—so if you're in Washington and you stop at the Lincoln Memorial, don't look for a family resemblance.

My parents brought me up in the Jewish faith. We lit the Sabbath candles every Friday night and they made sure I went to the Washington Hebrew Congregation religious school classes every Sunday morning. I always attended the High Holiday services with my parents.

We also had a monthly get-together with the entire family—

all the Wolfs, the Garners, all the cousins and aunts and uncles.

My paternal grandfather, Charlie Wolf, was from England. He came here with his family in the 1880s. His mother was Rachel Warshawsky, who was born in Poland. Her first husband's last name was Levy (we don't know the first name). We were always told that Levy, a diamond merchant who traveled from London to Johannesburg, South Africa, simply failed to return from one of his jewelry trips and was presumed to have disappeared. I might well have been Warner Levy but Rachel then married Wolf Quashne, who had been a friend of Levy's.

They were married in the Great London Synagogue in December of 1879. I acquired a copy of the marriage certificate on one of my trips to London. When Wolf Quashne arrived at Ellis Island with his family, they looked at his name and changed it to William Wolf. Thus, I became Warner William Wolf. Just think. How many guys could have been Warner Levy, Warner Quashne or Warner Wolf?

They chose Warner because it was the last name of Lyla Hanks' second husband, Ralph Warner. When I was growing up, the only two other Warners anybody had heard of were Warner Baxter, an actor and noted leading man in the movies of the 1930s, and Warner Brothers. Outside of that, it seemed no one else was named Warner.

I used to dislike my name. No one ever seemed to get it right. I told my father that one day and he said, "Son, someday you are going to be glad your name is Warner Wolf." And he was right. I am glad.

Because I was an only child, I was always very close with my father, although many of my earlier thoughts are also with my mother. She was meticulous, everything always neat and clean. No mess. And a very good cook, especially those Sunday dinners—chicken or matzoh ball soup, roast beef and mashed baked potatoes with peas or green beans. Or sometimes cold cuts—corned beef for me, tongue and pastrami for them.

I can also remember eating peanut butter sandwiches in the afternoon, lying on the floor in the living room and listening to the many radio shows—*Jack Armstrong, the All-American Boy, Captain Midnight, The Lone Ranger, The Green Hornet*—and the evening shows, that day's version of prime-time entertainment. Great stuff. Jack Benny, Fibber McGee and Molly, Fred Allen, Amos and Andy, *Inner Sanctum, Suspense, The FBI in Peace and War, Mr. Keen, Tracer of Lost Persons.* I used to listen to all of 'em.

The radio was also our gateway to sports. Boxing, baseball, football, scores and results. I heard 'em all. Little did I know at the time that this would become my profession, many years later. A guy named Tony Wakeman came on Washington radio every day for five minutes. He used to give the race results and any baseball scores. His theme song was "The Old Gray Mare." At the time he seemed very old to me. He was probably only thirty-five.

I do have one little complaint about my mother. When we used to go to dinner at a relative's home—usually my grandparents Charlie and Rose Wolf—my mother used to bring me my own milk from the house and cut my meat for me at the table. It was very embarrassing. I was eleven years old and she was still doing this. I guess I never wanted to hurt her feelings, so I never said anything.

When TV came along, my father bought us a Philco television with a three-inch screen. A big box filled with tubes and electronic gizmos but a tiny screen. So my father also bought a small, round magnifying bubble to place over the three-inch screen, then a larger, stand-up magnifying glass he put in front of the bubble. It made for about a ten-inch screen. But you had to view the picture head-on. It would be distorted from the sides. It was impossible for three people to watch the TV at once because you couldn't get three heads together straight-on. A far cry from these giant home entertainment systems you see today, huh?

National holidays were always big in my house, very significant. I was born on November 11, 1937—Armistice Day, now known as Veterans Day. My mother, Rosemary, was born on Labor Day in 1913. My father was born on July 4, 1909. My youngest daughter, Shayna, was born on Memorial Day, May 30, 1970. My parents were married on Thanksgiving in 1933. And my oldest daughter, Joy, was born August 30, 1960, Ted Williams' birthday (which should somehow be commemorated).

It's a wonder my name isn't Warner Holiday.

21

SERVING UNCLE

The only draft a young man has to worry about these days is in sports and there the pay is pretty good. When I was young, there was another draft and the pay wasn't much—the Army.

I loved my experience in the Army. I thought it was great. Served active duty in the Army Reserves from August 1960 to February 1961, followed by inactive duty, summer camp and reserve meetings for five and a half years, a six-year obligation.

My basic training took place at Fort Knox, Kentucky. Who would know that my first radio job would be in Pikeville, Kentucky, just one year later? Or that my wife, Sue, whom I would meet eight years later, would also be from the same Fort Knox.

For me, the best thing about the Army was that it taught you discipline and humility. If you don't learn that in the service, you have a very tough time.

Basic training ran ten weeks. Up at 5:00 A.M. and lights out at 10:00 P.M. Our sergeant was from Cuba. He used to say, "Gentlemen, by the time basic training is over in this man's Army, the overweight guys will lose weight and the skinny guys will gain weight. And remember this—you will always be hungry."

He was right. We were so active we always had an appetite. I remember one morning at breakfast when they served fried eggs. I never liked to eat the yolk. So I would cut around the eggs, eat the white part, and leave the two yolks on my plate. The mess hall sergeant came by our table, looked at my plate and said, "Eat those yolks or I'll make you put them in your pocket." I took a napkin in each hand, picked up each yolk, and put them in my pocket. The sergeant said, "Wise guy" and walked away. I was lucky on that one. But I actually thought the food in the Army was good.

The only thing that puzzled me a little was that while the Army insisted you wash your hands before every meal, you had to do five chin-ups on a huge overhead bar on your way to the mess hall. So here you had just spent time washing your hands and now you were gripping your hands all over the chin-up bar, where countless other hands had been. Once you were in the mess hall, it seemed nobody took the time to wash their hands again. You were too hungry. The sergeant was right.

There was one guy who wouldn't take a shower. His white T-shirt turned black. He really smelled. Nobody would get near him. Finally, someone told the master sergeant. He went after the kid, who was hiding under his bed and wouldn't let go of the leg of the bed. The sergeant, a round, stocky guy of about forty, dragged the kid into the shower and made sure he got clean. The kid never smelled again.

Bivouac was a great experience. You marched out of camp, full gear, for about twenty miles and stayed in the field for a week in a tent. Some guys had a tough time marching— they couldn't keep in step. The secret, of course: If you got out of step, you just skipped until you got in step. We had a guy named Zingle who was a nice fellow but just couldn't stay in step. The sergeant was constantly all over him. I can still hear him bellowing, "Zingle, get in step." For all I know, Zingle is still out of step.

I remember when we marched back at night after the week in the field was over—it happened to be a cold, rainy night— they had monster oil drums filled with hot soup for everyone. Man, we sat in the rain and ate that soup forever. I don't recollect what it was but in my mind it was the best soup I ever had.

Tell you another story about the Army teaching humility and discipline. One time everyone was issued new fatigue shirts. I picked mine up and, as usual, my sleeves were too long. Whenever I bought a shirt the sleeves were too long, so why should the Army be different? Unlike department stores, the Army has no complaint department. I asked the sergeant if I could have a smaller size in the sleeves. He said no, take the shirt and get out. After I tried to argue my case again, he said, "That's it. You will wash the sergeant's floors for a week. One more word and I'll add the latrines."

Great. The kind of work where you'd have to roll up your sleeves. End of my dispute.

After basic training, some of us went to Fort Sam Houston in San Antonio, Texas. I thought San Antonio and Fort Sam, as we called it, were terrific. Hot in the day, especially in October and November, but cold at night. It was there that I heard the ninth inning of the seventh game of the Yankees–Pirates World Series in 1960. We were all sitting outside on wooden bleachers and the instructor had a transistor radio. The ninth inning took about an hour, climaxed of course by Bill Mazeroski's home run. Isn't it funny how we remember where we were when certain historic moments took place?

One of the most difficult things to do was to stay awake at 7:00 A.M. during a lecture but even those early classes had their moments. There was a lieutenant who taught an anatomy class who was a graduate of Purdue University. He was very good and had a fast-moving delivery. We also noticed that, unlike many instructors, he never used a cuss word. In case you didn't know, there was a lot of swearing in the Army.

So one day he's showing us this big chart of the male body. He comes to the genitals. He says, "Gentlemen, these are the testicles. Better known as balls." It cracked everyone up. Suddenly, with no warning and as part of this educated, refined delivery, he just says "Balls." I still laugh about it.

That was mild compared to the outright cussing you would hear. We had this tough kid from New Jersey who couldn't say one eight-word sentence without six cuss words. He was, without question, the most foul-mouthed guy I ever met. It was just part of his everyday vocabulary. One night, long after the lights went out, he gets up to shut the window near his bed. The window falls and crashes down on his fingers.

He was in pain, but instead of just yelling for help, he begins every sentence with, "Come on you SOBs, get this

58

(bleeping) window off my hand. You (bleep-bleepers), help me, you (bleep) holes."

Everybody was laughing so hard at this guy, in obvious pain and needing help, who didn't know how to ask for assistance in a normal way. Nobody helped him at first. It was too funny.

Just before we were released in February from active duty, I was called into the sergeant's office. He informed me I was one of the ten guys who couldn't be released until I returned a library book I had taken out. I said I was sorry to say I never knew there was a library on base and had never gone. He then showed me a card and said, "See, it has your name on it. Wolfe—Thomas Wolfe." I said, "Sarge, that's the author of the book, not me."

When you are released, you are given airfare travel money, based on the flying mileage from the base to your home. I took the money and bought a bus ticket to Washington. I was in no rush, I got to see some of the country and made about $200 on the deal.

So I served Uncle Sam. And I enjoyed it. You never forget the camaraderie, the bonding, the people. You remember every Zingle one.

22

MEMORIES

It's funny what you remember from when you were a kid. It's not just the sights and sounds that overwhelm you but smells too. Scientists say the sense of smell is one of the most powerful links with certain memories in your life and I believe that's true.

I would go with my father to Senators games in Washington at old Griffith Stadium and the first thing you noticed was the great smell from the Wonder Bread factory on Seventh Avenue. It didn't matter, day games or night, you always smelled the bread from blocks away.

It gave you a feeling of the world you lived in, that all was right, but there was another heady fragrance I always associate with the ballpark—the smell of hot dog mustard. Go ahead, breathe deep. You can smell that tangy mustard in the warm summer air.

20/20 VISION

Welcome to the millennium. This major league turn of the calendar has people talking about all the changes in store for humanity and I, of course, am wondering what's ahead for sports. I'd like to take a look through my own personal time machine and hazard a few guesses what's twenty years down the road in the year 2020.

First prediction: All sports events will be sold and available via the Internet on your home computer. Any event, anywhere. Any time. You just punch it up at whatever.com and BOOM! And I predict there will be plenty to watch.

Instead of thirty-two NFL teams, thirty baseball teams, twenty-nine NBA teams and thirty hockey teams (that includes the three expansion teams added for the 2000–2001 season), there will be close to fifty teams in every sport—200 professional teams. And 175 of those teams will make the playoffs in their respective sports.

And that's not all that will be outsized.

Consider that in 1988 only 27 players in the NFL weighed over 300 pounds and by 1998 there were 250 players over 300. By 2020 all offensive linemen will weigh 400 pounds. Teams will bring in sumo wrestlers to plug up the middle against the run, so that 270-pound running backs (who will run the 40 in 4.0 seconds) can't break a big run.

In baseball, you can forget seventy home runs. With so many expansion team pitchers and the batters getting bigger and stronger—you won't find a first baseman under 6-9, 290—95 home runs and 200 RBI will become the standards.

The NBA? Forget it. The 7-foot player will be considered a midget, backcourt at best. Up front, no forward will be less than 7-8 and the center will have to be 8 feet tall or he won't be able to make it. (Already, going into the 1999–2000 season, there are 46 guys in the NBA over 7 feet tall; only 9 players are under 6 feet.)

In the NHL, the rink will suddenly be too small for the players, who will all be 6-6 and over. I predict you'll see the first 7-0 skater. The players may not be better but they'll be bigger.

And I boldly predict that the sports fan of twenty years from now will look back at Michael Jordan, Terrell Davis, Mark McGwire, Wayne Gretzky, and say none of them would have made it today. TOO SMALL!

24

LEAVE LIKE MIKE

As great as he was, I thought it was good that Michael Jordan retired when he did in January of 1999. I mean, it wasn't like he was calling it quits during his prime, in the middle of his career. After all, he retired one month short of his thirty-sixth birthday and played thirteen seasons.

It was also good because it gave other teams a chance to win the title. Only in basketball can one guy completely dominate the sport, which is what Jordan did. Scoring acrobatically, making clutch shots, especially the one that gave the Bulls their last title vs. the Jazz, lunging and making a steal, getting others to play above their level—that's what Jordan did, with a wonderful grace and a wagging tongue.

That's a dominant player. A make-a-difference player. Think about it. If Mark McGwire suddenly quit, would it affect the entire league, alter the pennant race, change the favorite to win the World Series? No!

If Jaromir Jagr suddenly retired, would the rest of the

NHL be affected? No. Certainly it would have a big impact on Pittsburgh, but not the rest of the league. If Randall Cunningham retired, would it change the NFL? Not likely. (And in fact the 1999 Vikings went on a midseason winning streak when Jeff George replaced him at quarterback.) Or how about Barry Sanders?

However, because a basketball team has only five men on the court at once and probably uses only eight players a night, one guy like Jordan can dominate the sport and really make a mark on the league. Baseball? No way. Too many guys, twenty-five players on a team. Even a great pitcher appears only once every four or five days. Did the Dodgers win the World Series every year they had Sandy Koufax? No. The NFL? Forget about it. There are fifty-three players on a team. Losing one player may hurt a team in that particular game but it won't vastly change the other thirty teams.

You can't deny how big a role Jordan played in Chicago's emergence as the NBA's preeminent team and as a worldwide attraction. He was truly one of a kind. But that's what they always say when a great one departs. It just makes room for the next big star.

Dr. J passed the torch (behind his back, on a bounce) to Magic Johnson and Larry Bird. Their era led to Jordan's. The NBA always survives the cycling in and out of stars.

There's a legend about to be born. There's always one coming along. Maybe it's Kobe Bryant, maybe it's Allen Iverson and maybe it's somebody not yet in the NBA. Like they say in telecommunications, just press the star key.

SHAQ

I'm at the gym one morning during the NBA's '98–'99 lock-out. I'm working out and I see Shaquille O'Neal doing his lifting and, believe it or not, practicing foul shots. I don't bother him.

But I catch up with him later in the locker room and I introduce myself to him and he says, "Sit down." It was like an audience with the Pope—a very big Pope.

He was putting money into this attempt to bring an NFL expansion team to Los Angeles and he was very involved, very tuned in to what the investors wanted to do.

He's convinced it will work, that the fans there aren't turned off to the NFL. He says they just didn't like the Raiders. I said, "What about the Rams?" They didn't like them either, or the stadium they played in down in Anaheim.

Shaq was in with a group headed by Michael Ovitz that the NFL liked. His group's plan was to put up a new stadium away from downtown, in Carson, with a mall and other sports-related entertainment.

Shaq was talking like a businessman, not like a basketball player. He took a lot of time, explained everything fully, but it left me with one terrible thought. He's such a nice guy, how'm I ever gonna criticize him again for missing his foul shots?

I would always go on the Imus show and say, "The Lakers lost 110–105. Shaq had a great night from the line, 2 for 11. Obviously if he had made six more foul shots, they could have won the game." You could say that about him almost any game. And now I'm going to have a hard time doing that. He was a nice guy! How can you pick on him? Even on the Imus show.

When he got up after our talk at the Reebok Club, this whole entourage came out of nowhere and all these people from the gym were following him out the door. He walked away, this big head above the crowd, looking like the Pied Piper.

He gets in the elevator, I'm with him, and this young lady stares up at him and I don't think she knew who he was. She says, "Man, you're tall." He looks down at her and says, "Yeah. And you're beautiful."

She must hear that all the time, but not from a 7-1, 300-pound guy.

By the way, Shaq and California didn't get the new franchise, which the NFL awarded to Houston.

WILTED

Dennis Rodman, released by the Lakers in April of 1999 after playing with the Pistons, Spurs and Bulls, would not be playing in his day, the late Wilt Chamberlain once told me. Not because of the tattoos, the strange behavior, the rainbow hair. Not that those would have been plusses.

Nope. Here's why. "We didn't have room for a one-dimensional player," Wilt said. "The guy only rebounds? Forget about it. He wouldn't make the team."

And these triple-doubles? "A guy today gets 10 points, 11 rebounds and 10 assists and they're all over the news," Wilt said. "If that's all Jerry West or Oscar Robertson did, it would have been a horrible night. Rodman gets 19 rebounds a game? I got 55."

In fact, with people complaining that Wilt could only score and rebound, he went out and led the league in assists during the 1967–68 season. That would be like telling Brett Favre to play defense.

"But these guys today," Wilt says, "they turn on the TV and they see only two things—dunks and three-pointers. You go to a playground and that's all you see. There's no pick-and-roll, no passing, the team concept is out and the individual situation is in."

I first met Wilt in 1965. Philadelphia was playing an exhibition game at old Uline Arena in Washington. After doing an interview with me, Wilt and I went outside and started walking down the street. Suddenly, a youngster about nine years old sees Wilt and says, "Hey, that guy must be on stilts." Little did the boy know that Wilt "The Stilt" was one of Chamberlain's nicknames.

27

LADIES' MAN

I asked Chris Evert if the number one woman tennis player could beat the 100th-ranked male player. Number one versus number 100.

She says, "The number one woman wouldn't beat the 350th-ranked male player and I know it. I played my ex-husband, John Lloyd, who was then ranked 350th, and he killed me every time. Speed, power, forget about it. He wiped me off the court every time we played."

In the fall of '98, I talked to Andre Agassi and he said virtually the same thing. "Look, this is not bowling," he said. "This is a power game and there's no way a female player is going to out-power a male player."

Have I just set up the New Millennium version of a Bobby Riggs–Billie Jean King match?

POINT, MR. McENROE

Remember that great Wimbledon match in 1981, when John McEnroe and Bjorn Borg were in their prime? McEnroe won the fourth set 18–16 but lost the match in five sets. Great match, July 4th weekend.

My wife is leaving for the beach but I can't go because I have to work. She tells me before she leaves, "Do me a favor. Don't go to Xenon. It's not a place for a married man without his wife." Xenon was one of those popular clubs in the '80s like Studio 54. So she asked me not to go while she was away and I said, "OK."

So I'm at work and Ernie Anastos, a TV anchorman in New York, says to me after the Monday night broadcast, "Hey, let's go to Xenon." I know right away this is going to be trouble. I say, "Ah, how about another place?" He says, "C'mon, I've never been to Xenon. C'mon, one drink and we'll leave."

I'm telling him no, I don't want to go, but he keeps insisting. Says we don't really have to go into the main part of the club, we can just stop at the back bar of the club and have one drink. One drink. OK.

So we go. We're at the bar. I swear we were going to have just the one drink, mind our own business and go home. Then, who walks in? John McEnroe.

Now, I had just done a piece on Wimbledon on the 6:00 P.M. and eleven o'clock news, saying McEnroe was the only guy on the planet who could stay with Borg today and that they are the class of tennis. McEnroe apparently saw the show. He comes walking over to me at the bar, sticking his hand out, and all of a sudden the flashbulbs start firing and the cameras are clicking. I don't know where they came from. I hadn't seen any photographers anywhere. I guess they followed him in.

The *New York Post* ran it the next day, huge pictures of McEnroe and me shaking hands in one of New York's hottest nightspots. All I could think of was my wife telling me not to go to Xenon, and there I am with McEnroe, getting press coverage. I had to call her up and explain.

Funny thing about the city. You go out for one little drink at a place you agreed to stay out of, and everybody in the five boroughs, Long Island, Westchester, Connecticut and New Jersey thinks you're a party animal.

29

HONEST TO PETE

I'm always amazed by the knock on Pete Sampras, that he isn't colorful or controversial enough. Is that so important? Who cares?

Were Rod Laver and Roy Emerson charismatic people? I don't think so, but, like Sampras, they were great tennis players who dominated their sport. Just because Ilie Nastase, Jimmy Connors and John McEnroe became colorful players with big-time, outgoing, demonstrative personalities doesn't have anything to do with Sampras, who rarely says anything on the court and lets his racquet do his talking.

Sampras may be the greatest singles player of all time, although you wonder how he would have done with a wooden racquet in tennis' earlier days, or how guys like Bill Tilden, Jack Kramer, Don Budge, Laver, Emerson and Ken Rosewall would have done with today's oversized, powerful racquets.

Colorful. Was Joe Louis colorful? No! That wasn't his personality. He just knocked everybody out.

Was Joe DiMaggio colorful? No! He just did everything gracefully. Were Jerry West or Oscar Robertson colorful? No! But they could move with the basketball, make pinpoint passes and clutch shots. They were great.

Now maybe McEnroe, Connors, Nastase and Andre Agassi spoiled it for everyone else. In this day and age of wall-to-wall highlights, maybe you have to also give people a show—besides winning. The fact is, women's tennis is now more popular than men's. There are more outstanding women players today than men. On any given night, the Williams sisters Venus and Serena, Martina Hingis, Lindsay Davenport, Monica Seles, Aranxta Sanchez Vicario, Anna Kournikova, Mary Pierce, and others could win a tournament. The competition is terrific.

But in men's tennis, it's Sampras and everyone else. Sure, the other guys—Agassi, Rafter, Todd Martin—can win. But when they do, it's considered an upset.

You know what hurts men's play? It's serve and BOOM! That's it. No volley. Game over. In women's tennis, the ball is in play longer. No wonder it's more popular. But don't penalize Sampras or attack him because he's so good at what he does and the way he does it.

LOOSE BALLS

Every sport has odd rules you wouldn't know about until something strange happens. Golf is loaded with them. Tennis has one that really bugs me.

I'm watching a match one night between Lindsay Davenport and Sandrine Testud. Testud wins the first set 6–4 and she's winning the second set, she's up 30–love, and she hits a ball which Davenport can't reach.

Davenport is running for this ball that she obviously cannot get to and a ball falls out of her pocket and onto the court. Can you guess what happened? According to the rule, there's no point and play is stopped.

Well, that's no good. A redo? C'mon. Change the rule. When the person who's about to lose the point loses a ball, she shouldn't get credit for a mistake like that. You can't reward a person who is about to lose a point. If the person losing the ball is about to win the point, well, OK, take it over. It's their fault. But you cannot reward someone for a mistake.

I'm certainly not accusing Lindsay Davenport of purposely dropping a ball out of her pocket, but you can see the problem here or what can happen. Someone about to go down 40–love could certainly drop a ball to stop play and keep from losing that point. As it so happened, Davenport did come back, won the set and went on to win the match.

Whoever came up with that rule really dropped the ball.

A DAY AT THE RACES

My signature at the end of every sportscast is the horse race. I started that about twenty-five years ago in Washington. We would always show the feature race at Laurel or Pimlico or Bowie and it was great. It only took the last ten seconds and, to make a bad joke, it paid off in on-the-air banter. It was good television.

You didn't need a big interest in the races to like it and sometimes you really got a good bit, like if the horses' names were funny or there was a big payoff. It gave you a little something to talk about coming out of the sportscast, it was something other people didn't do, and I've kind of been associated with it.

When I came to New York I did the same thing with Belmont, Aqueduct and Saratoga. Again, no one else did it so essentially the franchise belonged to me and that, I thought, was good. The people who watch you every day get accustomed to sharing that time with you and they buy into your style, whether it's colorful expressions or something like the race.

I went back to Washington for a brief period, 1992 to 1995, and we again picked up closing with the race. About two years into my contract, the news director calls me in and says, "Listen, I want you to stop doing the horse race." I said, "Well, geez, why?" He said, "I don't like the horse race. I don't think anybody does."

You don't think anybody does? Somebody's putting $2 on the nose of those horses. And here's the point I tried to make—we're the only one in town showing it. So no matter how small the audience may be for horse racing, you have that audience. You own it. They're not going to see it on the other channels. We're the only ones showing it and it's just ten seconds. It wasn't like we were showing a marathon, you know. We're picking up the race in the stretch, at its most dramatic point. It's a picture, a great moving picture.

Which is why I like it—the horses are pretty and it's a beautiful sight to see them run. The segment moves well. The payoff could be large, which gets people talking, and it's a way to bring the anchor people in at the end of the sports-cast. So I tell him, "I think it works." He says, "No, I don't want it."

Wow. I've done it for twenty-five years, for all these reasons, and here's a guy telling me his opinion is that he doesn't like horse racing, not even for ten seconds. He doesn't like it, nobody likes it and I can't show it.

I thought about it for a while and it turned out to be about the only time I ever went against a directive. He had come to me before the six o'clock news, around five, and as show time approached, my producer—Larry Duvall, a real nice guy—asked me, "What are we going to do with the race?"

So I said, "Let's run it." And we did. And the news director called me from home and said, "That's it, you're off the air."

For three days.

When I got back, I didn't run the races anymore. Picked it up again after he was let go a few months later and again of course when I went back to New York.

Some rebellion, huh? But I thought it was a poor decision based on little understanding of the business. This was something associated with me, important to me, and apparently important to some others. Got a letter from Jack Kent Cooke, then the Washington Redskins owner. He sent a copy to me and to the station, supporting me. He loved the horses, owned Elmendorf Farms, had a big house in the Virginia horse country. I know he wasn't the only fan of that ten-second closer. But sometimes you're at the mercy of one person's whim, which is one of the shortcomings and injustices of the business.

Personally, I don't go to the track that much—once a year to the Belmont Stakes. But I show it on the newscast because the horse race makes good television and I happen to be the number one fan of good television.

32

THE SPORT OF KINGS

Want to spend some time alone with your thoughts? Go to the racetrack. The place is empty.

Used to be the most popular spectator sport in the country. What happened? Off-track betting.

It would kill me that every year the *Daily Racing Form* would report that horse racing was the number one spectator sport. I would always come on the air and say, "Yeah, but suppose you took all the pari-mutuel betting booths out of the tracks? Hardly anyone would go just to see the horses run around the track."

Or I would say, "Suppose they put betting booths at NFL games, or at NBA or NHL arenas? Attendance would increase."

Horse racing is a betting sport. That's it. As long as people can go to an off-track betting parlor, the monster crowds are a thing of the past.

Sure, the Triple Crown races remain an attraction and there are a couple of other big days, like the Breeders' Cup. But now the tracks need slot machines to draw people in.

Can the sport recover? Don't bet on it.

SOCCER, OR GOOOOOOOOOO AWAAAAAYYYYYYY

Except for a short period of time in the late 1970s when the New York Cosmos put together a virtual all-star team to compete in the North American Soccer League, and the U.S. women's World Cup success in 1999, soccer just has never made it big in the United States. No question the Cosmos drew big crowds, but you have to remember some of the European and South American standouts they brought in— Pelé, Giorgio Chinaglia, Franz Beckenbauer, Carlos Alberto. That's why they could draw 77,000 to the Meadowlands on a Sunday afternoon.

So why hasn't this sport caught on here, when it's the world's favorite game? Well, I think it has a lot to do with American youngsters not growing up with the sport. For a sport to make it big in a country, it is vital that young people grow up with a hero playing that game. Like Pelé in Brazil, Johan Cruyff in the Netherlands, Roberto Baggio in Italy.

Those guys at home are like Michael Jordan here. Kids want to pretend they're Michael Jordan on the playgrounds, making that great move to the basket or a steal. Who does an American youngster growing up here pretend to be in soccer? No one. That's it. There's no market. Is anybody buying Ronaldo T-shirts here? I know there are lots of kids playing the game but that's because it's perfect for younger age groups, kids with lots of energy who don't want to stand around. But they have no home-grown idol.

Another thing holding back professional soccer and in fact the thing that might doom it is the time of the year the season takes place. The season coincides with the NFL, the NBA, the NHL or major league baseball. Soccer has no chance. In Europe and South America, soccer is the only game in town, with the possible exception of a little cricket and rugby.

Last—and again, except for the U.S. women's overtime win over China—there aren't too many Americans who can appreciate or want to see a 1–0 (that's one–nil to you soccer fans) or a scoreless game after ninety minutes. We just weren't brought up that way. Where's the equivalent of the long-ball home run or the sixty-yard TD bomb? Where's the three-point shot? In soccer there's just too much playing time and movement downfield that results in nothing. And Americans like results. We're the country of fast food—quick and move on. Immediate results.

Professional soccer has as much chance of making it big here as professional baseball would in Europe—none.

34

PUCK-NATIOUS

Before I moved to New York, I was never a huge hockey fan. Washington didn't get an NHL team until the 1974–75 season—The Washington Capitals. In fact, I did the TV color the Caps' first year. Hal Kelly of Toronto did the play-by-play. He was good, a real hockey man. But how bad were the Caps that year? We did forty games on TV and they won one.

You want to create more fans of the game? I've got a couple of proposals.

One I've pitched for years goes right to those who don't like fights. This one is easy. Drop your gloves and you're out of the game . . . and the next one as well. Why is it so important for players to drop their gloves? There would be no fights if players were required to keep their gloves on. You can't hold, hit and stand on skates at the same time with your gloves on. That's why they take 'em off. Well, I'm saying that as soon as your gloves are gone, YOU are gone.

Now, the NHL put in a good rule for the 1999–2000 season to stimulate more scoring in overtime: only four skaters for each team. But if the game is still tied after the overtime, then steal the Olympic rule and go to the shootout. Each team picks five skaters and they all have penalty shots, one at a time, until one team wins.

If you don't like the shootout, then the third suggestion comes from Oilers GM Glen Sather. Sather suggests NO points for a tie. Instead, it's all or nothing. Two points for a win, no points for a tie (obviously no points for a loss). His feeling is that if you're tied at the beginning of overtime (and you don't get any points for a tie), you are going to go all out for the win in overtime. Thus, more shots on goal. After all, under Sather's proposal, you literally have nothing to lose— if you lose.

35

LET'S WIN ONE

I love these hypothetical discussions based around some question guaranteed to start a fight.

Like: If you had to win one baseball game, who would be your starting pitcher?

It's almost impossible to pick. You can practically hear people shouting out names. Who could argue if you chose Koufax, Gibson, Marichal, Spahn, Seaver, Feller? You could take any one of these guys and not go wrong. How about Whitey Ford or Jim Palmer?

So we're arguing already. I can hear it. Different eras, different style of play, you name it.

The only way you could ever come close to being fair about this would be to say, Could I have this guy in a certain year? In other words, if I have to win one game, I want the 1968 Bob Gibson who was 23-9 and had an ERA of 1.12. Or I want Whitey Ford in 1961 when he was 25-4. Or Ron Guidry, the 1978 vintage, when he was 25-3 and had an

ERA of 1.74. Or Sandy Koufax of 1963, when he was 25-5 and had a 1.88 ERA.

There are just too many great pitchers to select from for one game and they had too many great years too far apart.

Same thing for football: You need one yard on fourth-and-goal from the one. Who gets the ball?

Some folks would say Jim Brown. Period. Well, what about Walter Payton or Barry Sanders (I know, the Lions didn't think he was a good short-yardage runner), or Terrell Davis?

Basketball. Who would you want to take the last shot? Jordan? OK. But how about Oscar Robertson, Jerry West, Larry Bird, Magic Johnson? The list goes on. When people tell you who they'd want for that last play, there are just too many great ones for anyone to tell them they're wrong.

Though of course that's just what everyone does.

So which ones rate on my chart?

Well, to get that one yard, I'd want Jim Brown. I saw him in his prime for nine years and he never missed a game.

A starting pitcher for one game? Two guys, please. For my right-handed starter I'll take Bob Gibson. The lefty? Whitey Ford. I grew up watching them. Gibson was unbeatable in 1968 and Ford had a career winning percentage of .690. Ford started the first game of no fewer than eight World Series. In 1960, for some reason, Casey Stengel did not start him in Game 1 against the Pirates. He started Art Ditmar, who lost 6–4. Ford pitched Game 3, shut out the Pirates 10–0 on a four-hitter. Then he pitched Game 6, which the Yankees won 12–0 on a seven-hitter. Stengel blew it. By not starting Ford until Game 3 (Bob Turley followed Ditmar in that rotation), the Yanks could only get two starts out of him, instead of three. They wound up outscoring Pittsburgh 55–27 but they lost, four games to three.

Stengel, who managed the Yankees to ten World Series appearances in twelve seasons, never managed another game for them. I have always felt that by not starting Ford in Game 1, as he had from 1955 to 1958, Stengel lost his job. As you know, the Yankees went to the World Series from 1961 to 1964 and Ford started Game 1 in each of those.

Finally, under the category "You've Got to Be Kidding!" in October of 1999, Major League Baseball announced its All-Century team: 30 players, as voted for through fan balloting, baseball executives, sports historians and members of the news media. To me, it's not who they picked but who they left out: How can Stan Musial, Tony Gwynn, Frank Robinson, Jim Palmer, Whitey Ford, Warren Spahn, Tom Seaver, Juan Marichal and Carl Hubbell not make the team? Granted, there are just so many roster spots and you can't include everyone. And I'm not saying to replace any of the players that were selected. But when you have a system that forces you to leave out at least seven of the greatest players of all time, there's something wrong with the system. Change the rules! Add more guys to the roster!

It would be like listing the 30 greatest actors of the century and leaving out Robert De Niro, Sir Anthony Hopkins and Jack Nicholson.

And then they picked a starting team from those 30 players, and the right-handed starter is Nolan Ryan. Granted, Ryan belongs in the Hall of Fame—but there's no way he starts ahead of Bob Gibson (251-174, 2.19 ERA), Bob Feller (266-162, 3.25 ERA), Jim Palmer (248-140, 2.78 ERA), Tom Seaver (259-143, 2.60 ERA), Juan Marichal (243-142,

2.89 ERA) or Walter Johnson (411-279, 2.17 ERA). Even with his 7 no-hitters, Ryan's record of 324 wins but almost 300 losses (292) doesn't compare with the other guys'. He only won 32 more games than he lost!

HALL OF RECORDS

When Mark McGwire hit 58 home runs in 1997 and Ken Griffey Jr. hit 56, a lot of people felt it was only a matter of time before someone would break Roger Maris' record of 61 set in 1961.

They didn't have to wait long.

Griffey hit 56 in 1998 but he was a distant third to McGwire's 70 and Sammy Sosa's 66. It prompted a lot of discussion about records that you just never think will fall.

I remember talking to Joe Torre in December of '98 about why he thought there were so many home runs hit that season. He didn't miss a beat. First, he said the ball was juiced up, that it was wound tighter so it would fly off the bats. Second, he said there is watered-down pitching. Also, the newly built ballparks are smaller, with dimensions reminiscent of the old days. And, finally, the players are stronger.

You've seen those Popeye forearms on McGwire. That tells you something. Today, players are encouraged to lift weights and come to spring training already in shape. Torre said that during his playing days, the players were told not to lift weights, that it was bad for you to become too muscle-bound and give up your flexibility. And players used to come in with the expectation of getting in shape during spring training, not being in shape to start spring training.

The home run chase got me thinking about a lot of those other records said to be unbreakable. I think a lot of those records set over the length of a career will probably stand the test of time and will not be broken.

How about Pete Rose's 4,256 hits? No. Simply because of today's salaries, no one will ever play long enough to accumulate that many hits. Rose played 24 years.

Cal Ripken's streak of 2,632 games? No again. For the same reason. Cy Young's 511 wins, Walter Johnson's 110 career shutouts, Hank Aaron's 755 home runs? No. You could hit 30 home runs a year for 25 years and still be 5 home runs shy. McGwire, Griffey and Sosa may be too old to last that long and approach the 755. Griffey, because he was only twenty-nine going into the 2000 season, would have an outside shot at Aaron's 755 but would still have to be hitting 40 home runs at age thirty-nine.

Single-season records are a different story. The one that may be tied but not broken is Johnny Vander Meer's back-to-back no-hitters. Ewell Blackwell came close, going 8⅓ hitless innings after throwing a no-hitter, but that's the closest to two no-hitters and it's doubtful anyone would pitch three no-hitters in three consecutive starts.

There's Joe DiMaggio's 56-game hitting streak, a testament to day-in, day-out consistency. True, Rose came close with 44 in 1978. But in DiMaggio's day, he frequently faced the starting pitcher four or even five times in a game. Today, with the specialization of the relief pitcher, who comes in fresh throwing 95 miles an hour, it's going to be harder in the late innings to get the hit that might extend your streak.

And when DiMaggio played, most of the games were in daylight. Today it's the reverse. Any player will tell you that it's easier to see a baseball during the day than it is under the lights at night. And then there's the travel. When DiMaggio played, for most of his career, there was no jet lag. The farthest trip from New York was to St. Louis—by train.

Unless the pitching gets even more watered down than it is now, you don't have to worry about who might hit in 57 consecutive games.

The funny thing is, after being stopped in the 57th game, DiMaggio went on to hit in another 16 consecutive games. So if he had gotten a hit in that 57th game (he was robbed twice by Cleveland third baseman Kenny Keltner), we would today be talking about DiMaggio's 73-game hitting streak, which would have been almost half of the 154-game schedule they played then.

Two other things about that streak. If he had hit in that 57th game, the Heinz company, with its famous 57 varieties, would have given DiMaggio a check for $5,000—worth about $100,000 today. Second, the Yankees won that game 5–4. However, when the game ended the Indians had the tying run at third. If they had tied the score, DiMaggio would have been up in the tenth inning with another chance to keep his hitting streak alive. You do know, of course, that DiMaggio did have a 61-game hitting streak in Triple A ball with the San Francisco Seals. DiMaggio told me that without question the earlier streak helped him deal with the 56-game streak years later.

In 1924, Rogers Hornsby hit .424. Could someone surpass that? Maybe. It will take a great hitter but it could be done. George Brett hit .390, Ted Williams hit .388 at age thirty-nine after hitting .406 sixteen years earlier at a youthful twenty-three. Rod Carew hit .388. A great hitter and diluted pitching make that record possible.

If there's an unbreakable baseball record, I'd say it's Hack Wilson's 191 RBIs in a 154-game schedule in 1930 with the Chicago Cubs. Let's do the math. Even with the 162-game schedule, no one has even come close. Not even 180 RBI or 170. To drive in 191 runs, a batter must have more than one RBI per game. If that's all he gets—and that's a great average—he's still 29 short of tying.

Throw in the slumps that even the best hitters endure and the fact that most players simply don't play in all 162 games and the odds get long. As the season drags through August and September, it gets tougher. And you can't drive in runs without men on base. You hit solo home runs, you get one RBI. I think this record can last, as long as the number of games in the season is not increased again.

Every sport has its enduring standards. And some may endure. Richard Petty winning 10 consecutive stock car races, for instance. Well, it could be that someone will match or surpass that, given the talent in racing and the better cars, but the competition is so fierce. How about UCLA's 88-game winning streak in college basketball? I don't think that one goes down. The players don't stay in school long enough to play together and form a dynasty. They move on to the pros in their sophomore or junior years now.

The Boston Celtics won eight NBA titles in a row. That's safe. Free agency will see to that. Plus, a team now has to win more playoff games than the Celtics did just to get to the championship series.

Wilt Chamberlain scoring 100 points against the Knicks, March 2, 1962. Could someone get 100? Could be. When Wilt did it, the game was played in the Hershey Hockey Arena. If you ever see film of this game—it's bogus! There were no camera crews in the gym. Rest assured if an NBA player gets 100, you'll see it.

The Lakers set a record for consecutive wins with 33 in 1971–72 and that record could be broken, with more expansion and more weak teams.

Think about Joe Louis holding the undisputed heavyweight championship of the world for twelve years, from 1937 to 1949. He didn't lose a fight. You're not going to see that again. Forget holding the title for twelve years. The money is so immense now from pay-per-view that the top guys lose their drive. Sure, they seem to fight forever after retiring several times, but you won't see one in his prime holding any title for a dozen years.

Or Sugar Ray Robinson going undefeated in 91 straight fights, from 1943 to 1951, after going undefeated in 85 amateur fights. 176-0? I don't think you'll see that again.

You remember the Chicago Bears scoring 73 points against the Redskins in the 1940 NFL championship, which they won 73–0. Will someone score 73 points again? Yes, though I can't say they'll win by 73. The Redskins scored 72 against the Giants in 1966, winning 72–41. The funny thing about the Redskins' 73–0 loss, if anything is ever funny in one of those, is that only three weeks earlier, also in Washington, the Redskins beat the Bears by the score of 7–3, with the Bears accusing the Redskins of pass interference in the end zone on the last play of the game.

I don't think you'll see anyone play 26 years of professional football the way George Blanda did. And—with all respect to Deion Sanders—I don't think you'll see anyone do what Bo Jackson did in 1989.

Bo made the All-Star team as an outfielder with the Kansas City Royals and also made the Pro Bowl as a running back with the Raiders. That's about the rarest double and one not likely to be repeated, because baseball and the NFL are not likely to let their players compete in another sport because of the huge financial investments they make in these stars.

One last thing: It bothers me when people talk about an athlete setting a new record. Of course he set a new record. You can't set an old one. You can only break it.

37

TEE FOR TWO

Except for that thrilling final round of the 1999 Ryder Cup, climaxed by Justin Leonard's 45-foot putt on 17, golf has to be one of the worst sports on television there is. To sit there and watch golf on TV for three or four hours? I'd rather take a walk. A long walk. It's just the worst, with the time these guys take between shots. Golf, an auto race and soccer are the last things I would watch on TV unless I had absolutely no choice. It would be like punishment to me. Hey, if you want to, show me the highlights. Sure. I show 'em. But the whole tournament, all day? What a bore. And they never enforce the rule about a reasonable time between shots.

In baseball, in a World Series game, a 3-2 count in the bottom of the ninth, the crowd is roaring. In golf? They have marshals telling the crowd, "Quiet, please" and holding up those little paddles. Like they'll swat you with them if you make a sound. I guess it's tradition. The concentration of a golfer would be broken if somebody yelled out just before a shot on a stationary ball, where a baseball player is just attuned to accept the roar from the stands on a ball moving 90 miles an hour and it doesn't affect him.

Take Braves closer John Rocker. Just before Game 1 of the 1999 World Series, Rocker was asked if he was worried or concerned about the New York crowd's reaction to him when the Series came to Yankee Stadium for Games 3, 4 and 5. "No!" he said. "Because when 55,000 fans are screaming at you all at once, it just sounds like one big roar. You don't hear any individual remarks. The problem occurs in a place like Montreal where there are only 5,000 people in the stands and you can hear the individual remarks." Ted Williams would agree with that. Referring to the excitement of getting up for a game, Williams said, "It's always easier to play in front of 50,000 people than 5,000."

I asked Tom Watson about it. Watson, of course, has won five British Open titles, two Masters and a U.S. Open.

"If the crowd cheered in golf the entire time, there would be no problem. If the crowd was silent the entire time, there would be no problem," Watson told me. "But if it's quiet and some sound comes out of the gallery, it could break the golfer's concentration."

Notice how everybody involved in golf uses the word "golf" over and over? The announcers, who always sound so reverential, insist on saying, "Excellent golf shot." What other kind of shot could it be in a golf tournament?

And for goodness sake, please tell us the length of the shot—excuse me, the golf shot. In baseball, we're told how far the ball went. In football, we know how long the play was and how many yards there were to go. In golf, we rarely hear an announcer say how far the ball went. Don't keep it a secret. Say it before the guy takes his shot. Not after or later during the wrap-up show. Tell us now, as he's lining up the shot.

Tom Watson broke in on the PGA Tour in 1971 and he's very candid in discussing the changes in golf and himself during his long career. I like that.

I asked him if he might have changed his game subconsciously as he began to win on the tour and the money began to pile up. He said, "When I first started, money was the motivation. If I made the top sixty that week, it meant I didn't have to qualify Monday. I just wanted to put money in the bank."

And he acknowledged winning changed his attitude.

"When I became financially secure and once I knew I was going to make money, I could then concentrate on just being the best golfer I could be," he told me.

He got to be pretty good. Five British Opens, two Masters, the U.S. Open, but never the PGA. He was pretty frank in remembering the PGA that got away.

"Hey, I had my shot in '78," he said. "I blew a big lead over the last nine holes and finished in a playoff with John Mahaffey and Jerry Pate and Mahaffey won. But that's the way it goes."

Nothing to be ashamed of there. Only four guys ever won all four—Jack Nicklaus, Ben Hogan, Gary Player and Gene Sarazen.

Golfers always talk about the front nine and the back nine but the real problem they face in their careers is their own backs. It is back injuries that have done in more of them than anything else. Two of them, Lee Trevino and Fred Couples, were good friends of Watson's. He told me that it stems from the pressure on the muscles and joints inherent in the golf swing itself. Golfers generate a lot of torque in whipping the club around.

"It's an unnatural swing," Watson said.

Torque is cheap. Trying to fix the problem so that they can have longevity, especially with the lucrative Senior Tour, has become important.

"Now, unlike years past, the players on the tour are working out. Fitness is priority number one," Watson told me. "It's not just the game anymore."

38

PRESSING ISSUES

Had the opportunity to get Mark Spitz and Carl Lewis to relive a little of their Olympic moments one afternoon. I couldn't help but ask them if there was any distraction stemming from the huge media interest in their chances at winning multiple medals. And they both agreed that they had paid little attention to what was being said and focused solely on the task at hand, thinking only about the event they had to compete in that particular day.

I know, it sounds like the old "take 'em one at a time." But there's a reason people say that.

Spitz said when he was winning his seven gold medals in 1972 in Munich that he was totally oblivious to the press and had spent the previous four years—after a disappointing performance in 1968—preparing for 1972.

Lewis echoed that. He said he only paid attention to the particular race he had to run at the time. He never looked ahead.

TENPINS

It amazes me how many people watch bowling on TV. Me, I find it hard to do, just like I have a tough time watching golf or auto racing on TV. It's just not for me. I'd rather watch an old movie.

Not that I don't like to bowl. In fact, as a teenager in Washington, we all went bowling at the Penn Bowling Alley in northwest D.C. It was a great place to take a date.

Washington was big on duckpins, those squatty little fat pins that you hit with a ball much smaller than the standard bowling ball. I don't know if that was a popular game anywhere but in Maryland and Washington and it's just about all gone now.

We used to tip the guys who set up the pins after each frame. There were no automatic pin setters in those days and the guys back there worked hard. They sat on a small perch just above the pins, and they'd clean 'em up, set 'em up and dodge the balls if people rolled them when they weren't ready.

My first recollection of bowling as a TV sport goes back to the early '50s—bowling from Chicago on Sunday night. The host, dressed in a suit, stood off to the side of the alley and would whisper as each bowler would approach the lane. Then his voice would get louder after the ball left the bowler's hand and got closer to the pins.

The bowler I remember best was Andy Varipapa, who had been around a long time, even then. He was about twenty-five or thirty years older than the other guys but always gave them a tough battle.

Would I watch bowling on TV now? No. Unless my wife, who is a good bowler with a 150 average, was in the tournament.

'98 SERIES DOESN'T RATE

I hate to say this but covering the 1998 World Series was a letdown. I was happy for the city of New York, the fans and the team, but as far as it being an exciting World Series, looking at it from a reporter's point of view, it just was not. Unfortunately, the Padres' manager, Bruce Bochy, took the Padres out of Games 1 and 3, the only games in which they had a lead and had a real chance to win.

As a result, there was never any doubt and the Series was won in four games. Four games. A sweep. Where's the drama? Where's the competition? Where's the matching of wits and skills? Missing, that's where.

I thought the turning point of the entire Series came in the first game when Bochy took out his number one guy—and certainly one of the best pitchers in baseball for 1998—with a 5–2 lead, two on and one out in the seventh. You yank Kevin Brown? No way. He should have let Brown pitch to at least one more batter, Chuck Knoblauch, a right-handed hitter.

True, Brown had been hit on the shin by a batted ball earlier in the game and had flu symptoms. But the point is, he was the Padres' number one guy and deserved a chance to pitch out of the inning himself. Plus, the Padres' middle relief had been terrible, even causing Bochy to bring in Brown in relief in the seventh inning of Game 5 against Atlanta in the National League LCS, rather than trusting his middle relievers.

As far as removing Brown because he had a knot on his shin and was feeling a little under the weather, just ask any old-time pitcher and you know what they'll tell you? They'll say, "Unless I can't raise my arm, I'm not coming out with a 5–2 lead in the seventh."

OK, maybe 5–3 or 5–4, but not 5–2. The worst Brown could have done would have been giving up a three-run homer to Knoblauch, which is exactly what his reliever, Donne Wall, managed to do. Let your ace do the work. He deserved a shot.

And how about being consistent if you're going to hook the starter? In Game 2, Bochy left his starter, Andy Ashby, in for 10 hits and seven runs (three unearned) before taking him out after 2⅔ innings. After the game, I asked Bochy why he waited so long in this shelling to take Ashby out. He said, "He needed innings."

Innings? He needed a *win*. What is there, another Series after this?

Bochy also said Ashby had the flu. But after the game, in the locker room, Ashby said it wasn't true and that he felt OK. Pitching coach Dave Stewart said he didn't know why Ashby was left in the game so long.

I was amazed none of the San Diego papers, nor any of the San Diego sportscasters, had criticized Bochy for taking Brown out of Game 1 prematurely and leaving Ashby in Game 2 too long. What a laid-back city. If Joe Torre had pulled the same moves and the Yankees were down two games to none, the fans would be booing and he would have been second-guessed by the print media, radio, TV and every New Yorker with an opinion, which is, of course, every New Yorker.

One big advantage of doing a live pregame show from the field at the World Series is you have so many great former players around, Hall of Famers—quality guys with a baseball pedigree. I went live with three Hall of Famers—Bob Gibson, Frank Robinson and Joe Morgan. Give me those old-timers any day. They obviously can be more outspoken than active players or any of the participants. And, unlike most of the younger players today, they know their baseball history. And just to show you the generation gap, when we told the producer of the 6:00 P.M. news we were going to have Hall of Famer Frank Robinson on, the producer said, "Who's Frank Robinson?"

Well, Game 3 didn't turn Mr. Bochy into a strategy whiz either. To his credit, he was a stand-up guy and he answered all the postgame questions, but he again made a questionable move. Trailing 5–4 in the last of the ninth, he used John Vander Wal, his best left-handed pinch hitter, as a pinch runner. As a result, with runners on first and third and two out, he had to stay with Andy Sheets, a right-handed hitter, who struck out to end the game.

When asked why he used Vander Wal as a pinch runner and didn't use lefty hitter Greg Myers as pinch hitter in the ninth against Mariano Rivera, Bochy said he felt his right-handed hitters were getting better swings against Rivera than his lefties. No point in playing percentages here, right?

To complete the series of questionable moves, we go to Game 4. Padres trail 1–0, with the Yankees batting in the top of the eighth, one out and the bases loaded. Bochy brings the infield in against Scott Brosius, the Series MVP. Well, here's the Yankees' hottest hitter but also one of their slowest runners. The Padres' best chance to keep it a one-run game is to hope for Brosius to hit into a double play, considering Ricky Ledee, who was four-for-five against Brown, is on deck. But the Padres brought the infield in. As Casey Stengel once said, when you bring the infield in you turn a .200 hitter into a .300 hitter. The odds increase big-time for the batter to get a hit with the infield in. It wasn't like Brosius needed any extra help here.

The result? Brosius hits a short pop fly just over shortstop Chris Gomez' head. That ball undoubtedly would have been caught by Gomez had he been playing at double-play depth. Instead, it went for a 95-foot RBI single and Ledee followed with a sacrifice fly to make it 3–0, which was the final score.

After the game, I asked Bochy what the thinking was in bringing the infield in. He did not respond at first and just looked at me. So I added, "Since Brosius was a slow runner you might have had a chance for a double play if the infield was back instead of in."

This time he answered. He said, "Well, the infield wasn't all the way in. We've done that some this season."

And now his season was over.

I thanked him and left the interview room to go to the field and the clubhouse to tape the Yankee postgame interviews for the next day and that was something I looked forward to. It was amazing. The Yankee players had come out on the field after the game to thank and recognize the 10,000 Yankee fans who had made the trip to San Diego and the emotion was so genuine and overwhelming. The Yankees washed away any hint of the self-centered athlete.

Of all the postgame comments from all the players I interviewed, I thought the most interesting one came from Andy Pettitte, the winning pitcher. Pettitte, who to that point was 0 for 10 as a batter, had to hit for himself in the National League park because they don't use the designated hitter. He struck out with the bases loaded against Kevin Brown in the second inning.

I asked Pettitte about striking out and he said it was amazing to stand at the plate on the other end of a major league heater. He said he didn't realize how fast Brown's ball came in there. He said he could see it coming and thought he had a bead on it. But he would swing and the ball was by him. American League pitchers rarely bat. They only see the ball from their perspective on the mound, going away from them, toward the batter. Seeing it come toward him, rocketed at him by one of the fastest pitchers in the game, was an entirely different experience, Pettitte said.

Say what you want about the difficulty factor in performing any of the feats in sports, but as Ted Williams always said, "There's nothing more difficult than hitting a baseball."

It's funny. I felt bad for Bochy and the Padres. I was hoping they would win at least one game. But you know what? It didn't seem to bother the Padres fans. They were just happy their team made it to the World Series. It was like they didn't know they'd been swept. As far as they were concerned, Bochy could have been made manager of the year. In fact, he was—according to some of the news services. What a tale of two cities, huh? In New York he'd have been roasted, not toasted.

On my flight back to New York from San Diego the next night, the movie was—of all things—*The Joe Torre Story,* starring Paul Sorvino. It was the story of the '96 championship Yankees and about Joe and his brother Frank's heart transplant. The flight attendants came around offering headsets for $5.

Strange, but I didn't see a single person buy the headset. Maybe because they had just seen the real thing—the 1998 version.

41

YANKEE DOODLINGS

Were the '98 Yankees the greatest team of all time? The '99 Yankees? Who's to say? But that's what makes baseball. People talk baseball like no other sport. It has a history extending back past the Civil War. It's sewn into the American fabric. It's part of us and it ties in with our other national pastime—arguing.

You want to get a good dispute going, just ask somebody to name the greatest team of all time. Good luck. Your Yankees fans, after that wonderful season, no doubt will make a pitch for the '98 Yanks—Derek Jeter, Paul O'Neill, Series MVP Scott Brosius, Mariano Rivera. But how about the '75 or '76 Reds, with Morgan, Bench, Rose, Foster, Griffey, Perez? Or the '71 Orioles—Frank Robinson, Brooks Robinson, Boog Powell, Palmer, McNally, Cuellar, Dobson, a pitching staff of all 20-game winners? Or the Oakland A's of the early '70s, with Catfish Hunter, Fingers, Reggie, Vida Blue, Kenny Holtzman?

Or take the nostalgia trip. The '27 Yankees—Gehrig, Ruth, Lazzeri. Connie Mack's 1929 Philadelphia A's—Foxx, Simmons, Cochrane, Lefty Grove. You could go on and on when you start to measure the great teams from all eras against each other. Take your pick. The point is, it's a great discussion.

The only thing that I think is a little unfair is that a lot was made of the Yankees winning 114 games in the regular season, 11 more in the playoffs, which is great. The playoff grind is as tough or tougher than the World Series. But the fact is, a team like the 1954 Cleveland Indians, for example, won their 111 games in a 154-game season. The Yankees played 162. What would have happened had the Indians played eight more games? A split would have put them at 115. Five out of eight would have allowed them to tie the Cubs' all-time record of 116.

Maybe the standard of 125 victories can be surpassed but how can you compare that with the 1906 Chicago Cubs, with 116 regular-season plus two World Series wins. How can you compare that with the Yankees when the Cubs played 10 fewer regular-season games (152) and no playoff games before the Series. I don't care about the 1906 Cubs but the point is, if you're going to make the Yankees the winningest team of all time (seven more than the Cubs), then give them the benefit of playing 10 more regular-season games and 7 more in the postseason. Come on.

If the Cubs only split their last 10 and won 7 playoff games like the Yankees, they'd be at 130.

I will say this: If the 1906 Cubs played the 1998 Yankees, the Yankees would sweep 'em easy. Those Cubs guys would be about 120 years old.

42

THE METS BLUNDER

In my twenty-six years as a sportscaster in New York City, I never saw a worse public relations move by any sports organization than the one the New York Mets pulled in February of 1999. Without any warning, the Mets simply dumped their fine TV analyst Tim McCarver—who's only the best in the business—and hired Hall of Fame pitcher Tom Seaver in his place. Their fine PR man, Jay Horowitz, had nothing to do with it, although the move did come from very high up in the Mets organization.

Sometimes you can give an organization the benefit of the doubt, but here there was no doubt. First of all, McCarver was entering his seventeenth year in the Mets' booth. He's the best baseball analyst of our time. He is not only on top of the game—enough to be a manager himself—he's also wonderful at making a point about a play before it happens. He doesn't have to second-guess.

The beautiful thing was that he was good at what he did

and apparently had free rein to criticize the club when the situation called for it. Well, that seemed not to sit well with someone in the Mets' family. And that was it for McCarver.

If the first blunder by the Mets was letting McCarver go, the second was to bring in Seaver—as not just a broadcaster but also as a member of the front office in marketing and as a pitching instructor. What in the world were the Mets thinking? How could Seaver be on the air making pointed comments about a pitcher that he was also giving advice to? If the pitcher allows a home run, what's Seaver supposed to say—"I told him not to throw that pitch in that situation"? Or, better yet, "Gee, I guess I was wrong. That's what I told him to throw."

Come on. That's called a conflict of interest. You can't put an active coach on the air and ask him for unbiased analysis.

The third gaffe was to think that George Steinbrenner would not capitalize on the situation and hire McCarver for the Yankees' announcing team. Which he did, very quickly. With the Yankees receiving more headlines than the Mets, the Mets did not have to help the Yankees grab even more positive attention.

To my mind, it was and is the all-time lame-brain public relations decision.

However, I will say this: As the season progressed, with the Mets playing very good ball—even making it into the NLCS against the Braves—the loss of McCarver was forgotten by many Mets fans.

THE CHAIN OF COMMAND

As you know, TV and radio are two of the most competitive fields around. Which is great for the performer. It should give him or her incentive to hustle, to be better than the next person. One of the ways is to get a story or a sound bite from an interview you did that no one else has.

In the early summer of 1997, Hideki Irabu made his American pitching debut. My news director sent me and a producer, Nick Juliano, to Tampa for the game. Irabu was going to pitch for the Yankees against their Class A minor league team, the Tampa Yankees. Before the game, on our first broadcast at 5:20 P.M., Nick and I lined up an interview with George Steinbrenner, who had invested $13 million in Irabu. It was a little like the opening out of town of a Broadway show—and Steinbrenner was the producer.

We tried to call the station on our cell phone but it wasn't working. And then, at the last minute, Steinbrenner told us he couldn't go on the field, but if we wanted to tape the interview we could meet him in his private office at 5:10 P.M. Nick and I rushed to the office with our cameraman and finished the interview by 5:15. We had no time to call the station and barely enough to do the interview with George.

Nick took the tape and had to run downstairs to the dugout and then run to an area out beyond left field to pass the tape on to the satellite truck for transmission to New York. I had to race downstairs and get on the field for the 5:20 live shot. And we both made it. Real television—the way it should be.

The interview was right on the money! We had Steinbrenner saying, for the first time, that if Irabu didn't succeed, it would be his—Steinbrenner's—fault and he would take sole responsibility. It was terrific TV and exactly what TV is all about. We got the news on the air on time and it was a scoop, because whenever a deal didn't work out, George would say it was the fault of his "baseball committee."

The only unfortunate thing is that at the time the executive producer back in New York didn't know we had Steinbrenner. But if we had stopped at a pay phone, we never would have made the show and the interview would not have made it on the air.

The bottom line: Get the piece on the air on time and explain it later. In the '60s, '70s and '80s, it would have been called good TV. In the '90s, in this case, going through the proper channels was more important than the final product.

Once in a while, you have to question the news judgment of your superiors.

In the summer of '98, the Mets signed Mike Piazza from the Marlins. I called in on my way to work to tell the executive producer I should go right to Shea Stadium and do the 6:20 sports from the ballpark. This is news, big news, and the approach should be obvious. Go out to Shea, interview manager Bobby Valentine, GM Steve Phillips, and Todd Hundley, the catcher Piazza would eventually replace.

The executive producer said, "I can't send you to Shea. You won't be able to do the play of the day."

The play of the day was a thirty-second piece that ran at 5:50. He told me the logistics were wrong for getting our cameras from the Mets' interview room, where a press conference would be held, to doing the play of the day at 5:50, and then back to the field at 6:20.

I said, Forget the play of the day. The story is Mike Piazza coming to the Mets, and live from the field at 6:20 is the place to be. He said we couldn't do it, because we would have a thirty-second hole to fill at 5:50.

I couldn't believe I was having this conversation with the executive producer of the station, who was being paid to know what was going on. I finally told him his priorities were off and that if we didn't go live at 6:20 from the field, we would be the only New York station not broadcasting live from the field.

He put me on hold. I don't know who he spoke to but he finally got back to me and told me to go to Shea.

It was the only story in town, as they say. I shouldn't have had to sell it.

Or the time last October when I'm going on the air to do the 11:25 sportscast during the final game of the Mets–Braves playoffs. The producer calls me in the sports office, says, "Don't give the score of the Mets–Braves game"—which was 8-8 in the 8th at the time. I said, "Hey, I'm a sportscaster, how can I go on the air and *not* give the score of the lead story in New York?" He says, "If you give the score you'll remind people that the game is on." I told him, "Anybody that is interested *knows* it's on and is already watching. You're not going to lose any viewers to the game just because I give the score."

To his credit he agreed. I gave the score.

Another time, just before the 11:00 P.M. news is about to begin, former middleweight champion Rocky Graziano dies in Manhattan. Rocky, a hard puncher and a colorful guy, appeared frequently with Martha Raye on TV in the 1950s. He was middleweight champ for one year after knocking out Tony Zale in 1947 in the second of their three great fights.

The 11:00 P.M. show's producer leads with the story, having the anchorman do it—and shows, by mistake, film of Rocky Marciano. At least he didn't show Rocky Balboa!

I have always felt that if you are to be a successful producer of the six or eleven o'clock news, or the executive producer of all the news shows, you should have knowledge of all fields, including sports.

Now, the point of all these examples is not to criticize the news director, producer or executive producer—and it is usually not a good idea to go over their heads. However, for all you potential sportscasters out there, always remember this: It is *your* face the audience sees, not theirs. If it looks bad, it is *you* who looks bad, not them.

You are the direct connection between the station and the audience. You are being invited into the people's homes.

Make the best of it.

44

THE NEW GEORGE

I've known George Steinbrenner since I first came to New York in 1976 to do the local six and eleven o'clock news on WABC, Channel 7. He had purchased the team three years earlier from CBS for about $10 million when the Yankees were a mess.

One thing you have to say about him, unlike a lot of other owners—when the Yankees need a player at a certain position, he goes out and gets 'em. He really is a fan's owner.

It's possible the fans in New York are spoiled because they take it for granted that George will just go out and fill whatever voids there are and put a competitive team on the field. Not living in another city, some Yankee fans probably think that's the way it is everywhere. Obviously, it isn't.

Well, I must say I was not crazy about George for a long time. I thought he was an egomaniac who never accepted the blame if he made a bad deal. Like I pointed out, he was always saying it was his baseball committee that had the final say. The other thing I disliked about him was that he always chastised his players and coaches through the media, rather than behind closed doors. I just thought that was plain wrong.

I remember in 1977 Reggie Jackson, who had been a pretty good right fielder, was misjudging balls left and right, especially in night games. George came on one of our morning live TV shows at Channel 7. I suggested that Reggie needs glasses. George was adamant. No, all our players have their eyes checked periodically, he said. Two weeks later, Reggie's in the outfield, wearing glasses.

When I came back to New York in 1997, I found a different George Steinbrenner. This guy has really mellowed. I don't know if it's age or a change of life but he's not the guy I remembered from when I left. Every time I see him now he puts his arm around me and says, "Let's go to the videotape."

In the pressbox before Game 1 of the '98 World Series, he pulls out a letter from Bill Parcells and shows it to me. It said, "I admire the way you stick to your beliefs. Don't change because of outside influences. That's the key to success."

I thought it was very nice that he would share that with me. I said, "George, this is what it's all about. It doesn't matter whether you win or lose the World Series, it's getting into the Series that counts."

You probably couldn't have said that to him ten years ago. Know what he said to me? "You're right. Look at the Knicks. Look at the Rangers."

I saw him again in the clubhouse after Game 4, after the Yankees finished the sweep of the Padres, and the guy was like a fan, like it was the first time he had ever won. He was not aloof, or CEO-like. He took my microphone and said he didn't know if this was the best team of all time, but it was the best team he had ever been associated with.

By the way, speaking of Irabu in the previous chapter and Steinbrenner's call in taking responsibility for his performance: After three seasons with the Yankees, Irabu was 29-20. However, in spring training of '99, in two consecutive games, the Japanese pitcher failed to cover first base on ground balls hit to the right side, with the result that Steinbrenner called him "a fat toad." A few days later I went on the Imus show and said, "This just in: George Steinbrenner has apologized to Hideki Irabu, saying Irabu is not *fat*."

For the record, in Game 3 of the 1999 ALCS between the Yankees and Red Sox, Irabu threw 4⅔ innings of relief, giving up 13 hits and 8 runs—a playoff record for relievers. He was not included on the Yankees' World Series roster.

45

INFLATION

I can just imagine Mickey Mantle and Roger Maris rolling over in their graves. For the 1999 season, Astros infielder Tim Bogar, who hit .154 in '98, signed a two-year deal averaging over $500,000 for each season. Braves pitcher Mike Remlinger received over $1 million for the '99 season after going 8-15 with an ERA of 4.82 in '98.

Nothing against Bogar and Remlinger. Good for them, if they can get it. If that's what the market offers, you can't begrudge them for taking it.

My point: Prior to expansion in 1961, when you had only eight teams in each league, if you were an infielder who only hit .154, or you were a pitcher with an 8-15 record and allowed almost five runs a game, there was a pretty good chance you wouldn't be around next season.

The 8-15 pitcher may have had a shot if he was pitching for a bad ball club like the St. Louis Browns, but the .154 hitter would definitely be gone. Obviously you had to be better when there were only 400 major league players, compared to 750 today.

Expansion is just another way of saying more minor league players, especially pitchers, are now playing in the major leagues.

46

TONY, TONY, TONY

I had always been a great admirer of Tony Gwynn—eight-time National League batting champion, future Hall of Famer. I always had the feeling that, except in San Diego, he was almost a secret.

When I approached him at the '98 Series for a television interview, I began with, "Tony, you are one of the greatest hitters of all time, eight times the batting champion, future Hall of Famer" and with that he turned to a group of writers surrounding us and said, "Wow! Did the rest of you guys hear that? Thank you, thank you."

With that reaction I felt he was exactly proving my point. As great as he has been over his seventeen-year career, his recognition factor, except in San Diego, is not high. Not around the country, certainly.

So I said, "Tony, have you ever thought how your career would have changed if you had been playing in New York all these years?"

He said yes, he had thought about it many times, and he probably would have been much more well known. But, he said, that's not what he's about. He said he doesn't like the limelight and being in the forefront, and playing in San Diego affords him the opportunity to stay that way. He liked being at home. Remember, he played college ball at San Diego State and his wife is from San Diego. He called himself a laid-back guy who loved the San Diego style of living. That's why he has stayed with the Padres all these years.

Obscurity equals privacy, I guess. You don't get much of that in New York if you're an athlete or, for that matter, a high-profile performer of any type. The pace is much faster, the interest level much deeper and the public is just a whole lot more curious about every aspect of your life. You eat at a fine restaurant, it's on Page Six of the *New York Post*. You go to a bar, it's in the *New York Daily News*. That's the way it is. People want to know you, or about you, and they're insatiable if you're a high achiever in sports. You can have no secrets. Single guys like Derek Jeter and Mike Piazza don't go anywhere without somebody writing about it.

So for Tony Gwynn, he made the right decision. Those are his values. But I can't help thinking about what his place in baseball history might be had more people seen him play and gotten to know him. Horace Greeley must have had Tony Gwynn in mind when he said, "Go West, young man." Or, in Gwynn's case, *stay* West.

47

AN ORDER OF RIBBIES AND A FULL PLATE OF BASEBALL

Hank Aaron hit 755 home runs. Everybody knows that. Broke Babe Ruth's record, became the greatest home run hitter of all time, showed the mental toughness, with people hating him, rooting against him for all the wrong reasons, to keep on doing what he did.

So you'd think Hank Aaron would be proudest of that record, of all those home runs. Right? Wrong! You'd have misjudged that man and what was really important to him.

I talk to Hank, I say, "How important were the home runs compared to the RBIs?" No comparison. It's the RBIs that count. That's what Hank said. He said, "You're more valuable to the team with the RBIs. Anybody can hit a home run. It's RBIs. And that's what I'm most proud of—more RBIs than any player in the history of baseball."

We also talked about longevity. You know, he played twenty-three years. He said, "You'll never see that ever again. No one will ever play twenty-three years."

I say, "Why?"

He says, "Because it took me twenty years to get $100,000. That's why you'll never see it today. An average ballplayer makes $2.5 million. Why's he going to play twenty-three years?"

Aaron, you might not know, actually hit 756 home runs. One of them was called back. In a game against the Cardinals, Aaron hit one out of the park. As he started to round first base, the first base coach said, "Hank, I think the ump is calling you out."

Aaron told me that it was the closest he ever came in twenty-three years to being thrown out of a ball game. The umpire, Chris Pelekoudas, said Aaron reached out and stepped over the plate from the batter's box to hit the ball, which is an automatic out. Aaron said he couldn't believe he had been called out.

If that home run had been allowed, home run number 714 hit in Cincinnati would have been 715 and the one in Atlanta, which broke the record, would have been anticlimactic as number 716.

Another thing Aaron told me was that he was originally included in the Bobby Thomson–for–Johnny Antonelli trade in 1954, with Thomson going to the Braves for Antonelli as the key players in the deal—but the Braves changed their minds at the last minute. Can you imagine that? The Giants would have had Willie Mays in center field and Hank Aaron in right! Thomson, by the way, broke his ankle in spring training with the Braves.

No. 7

Tell ya a story about Mickey Mantle. Nineteen fifty-six. He wins the Triple Crown, hit .353, 52 homers, 130 RBIs. Guys used to get paid on what they did the previous season, so at the end of '56 he gets a raise to $100,000. In 1957, he hits .365, 34 homers and 94 RBIs and goes into Yankees general manager George Weiss for a raise. And Weiss says, "Not only don't you get a raise, you get a cut." Mantle says, "How come?" "You didn't win the Triple Crown. You didn't even win the batting title." Mantle says, "Win the batting title? Ted Williams hit .388. How'm I supposed to win the batting title?" So Weiss takes a different approach, hands him a contract and says, "Sign or we'll trade you to Cleveland for Rocky Colavito." That's the way it was. And Mantle later told me, "Hell, I didn't want to go to Cleveland."

Besides Yogi Berra, Mickey, looking in from center field, was the guy who probably had the best vantage point for the final strike in Don Larsen's perfect game in the '56 series. You know, there was a lot of controversy about whether umpire Babe Pinelli, in his last major league game behind the plate, called a high pitch to Dale Mitchell strike three to nail down that piece of history. I said, "Did you think it was a strike?" Mickey said, "I don't know, Yogi had to jump so high for it, he blocked my view."

A Pain in the Asterisk

I interviewed Roger Maris in 1985, the year he died. We talked about the asterisk that the commissioner at the time,

Ford Frick, had put on his record of 61 home runs. Roger said the thing that bothered him was that, counting walks, when he hit his 60th home run he had only six more at bats than Ruth. And you know Frick was Ruth's buddy, his biographer. Maris hit 61 home runs, drove in 142 runs, MVP. Nice guy, misunderstood. He was a good speaker, maybe too honest about his feelings for the press of that time. Those guys ate him up.

Moose Skowron told me that Maris was so low-key, they had to push him out of the dugout to take a curtain call after his 61st home run.

Big Mac

Seventy. Seventy home runs. Even now it's hard to believe Mark McGwire hit that many, broke Roger Maris' record by nine. But you know what impressed me about that? It was the way McGwire went about it, his sense of history and the way he approached his task.

That season, the Cardinals came to play the Mets in August and he had 49 homers. I said, "Mark, you said that there was no point in talking about 60 home runs, no point in getting serious about it, until someone had 50 with a month to go." I said, "You have 49 and it's the middle of August. Assuming you hit one more in the next two weeks, will you then start to get serious?"

And he said, "I always felt that was the way it was, even when I was in high school. You have to have 50 home runs by September 1 to mentally and physically have a shot at 61 home runs."

From that point on he hit 21 more home runs. And people rooted for him to break the record. It saved baseball, to me. No question. The Yankees won a record number of games and went on to sweep the Padres in the World Series, but the thing that people talked about, the thing that captured them, was the home run race between McGwire and Sosa. The non–baseball fan talked baseball, became interested. And showing the home runs on TV didn't hurt either.

The Way It Used to Be

Why do you have players making millions of dollars a year? Blame the owners. Not just for paying the players millions, either. This is all their fault, going back to the very beginnings of professional sports.

They were so one-sided, with their petty rules and their nickel-and-diming of players, not allowing them to have agents, giving them a dollar or two and then taking it back. When it began to turn, it turned 180 degrees. The players gained the leverage and they've showed no more mercy than the owners did.

Brooks Robinson once asked Harry Dalton, the Orioles GM, for a $500 raise. Not $5,000, $500. Harry says, "Brooks, I'm not going to give you that raise." Brooks says, "Harry, I want $500. That's it, $500."

So Dalton tells him, "Brooks, I'm going to leave the room for five minutes and I want you to reconsider this." He leaves, comes back in five minutes and says, "So, Brooks, what's your decision?"

Brooks says, "Harry, I want the $500."

Dalton stops, then says, "All right, Brooks, I'm gonna give

you this $500. But let's just go on the record that you took advantage of me."

Hey, 1954, Duke Snider hits .341, 40 homers, 130 RBIs, he's making $40,000, he wants $55,000, a $15,000 raise. Dodgers owner Walter O'Malley says no, gonna give you a $7,000 raise. Snider says, "I hit .341, 40 homers, 130 RBIs." O'Malley says, "Yeah, but your stolen bases dropped from 16 to 6." He got a $7,000 raise.

Or Warren Spahn. Wins 363 games, top salary was $87,500. In 1963, he's forty-two years old, he goes 23-7. He goes to Braves owner Lou Perrini and says, "You know, I think it's time I got a raise."

Now this is after he's won 20 games or more six years in a row, and Perrini tells him, "You're supposed to win 20 games."

So Spahn asks him, "So how do I get a raise?"

Perrini says, "Win 30 games."

Not to sound like Walter Cronkite, but that's the way it was.

The Scooter

It's his rookie year, 1941. The Yankee Hall of Fame shortstop Phil Rizzuto hits a home run at Yankee Stadium to beat the Red Sox, first home run of his major league career. Now at the time, according to Rizzuto, it was not uncommon for a fan to run on the field and grab the player's hat.

So Phil's telling me this story and he says, "I'm running around the bases and I'm very excited because I know I'm not a home run hitter and it wins the game. And a fan comes running out and takes my hat. I don't think about that at all.

I go into the clubhouse. I call my folks and tell 'em about the homer, and I'm really enjoying this."

Well, he comes in the next day and the clubhouse attendant tells him, "Mr. Barrow wants to see you." That's Ed Barrow, the general manager of the Yankees.

Barrow calls him, says, "Sit down, young man."

Rizzuto waits. Barrow looks at him.

"Young man," Barrow says, "this is the major leagues. You were very careless with your equipment. That hat will cost you $6.50."

Joe D

Nowadays an athlete can't go anywhere without being recognized. People see your face on TV, boom, they feel like they know you, come up and shake your hand, recognize you in the airport. Very different from the past.

One year in the off-season, Joe DiMaggio was going to receive an award at a dinner in Iowa, he's got a driver and they're lost on their way to Des Moines. In the middle of nowhere. Farmer comes up to the car, sticks his head in the passenger window where Joe is, the driver says, "We're lost, we're trying to get to the main road. Can you help us?"

Farmer says, "Yep, just down the road, make a right, go about ten minutes, you'll hit the highway."

Pulls his head out of the window, starts to walk away. Then he turns back and says, "Oh, hi, Joe."

I sat next to DiMaggio at a dinner in New York at the Waldorf in the mid-'80s and he recalled an incident in the 1936 World Series. He said that on the final out of the last game—the Yankees beat the Giants in six games—he made a running catch of Hank Leiber's long fly ball at the Polo Grounds. "After the catch, I continued to run straight up the outfield steps, leading to the clubhouse," Joe told me.

But then he remembered an announcement made two innings before that asked everyone, including the players, to please stay on the field at the conclusion of the game to allow President Roosevelt's motorcade to drive across the field and leave through the centerfield exit.

DiMaggio said he froze on the first step, with the ball in his glove.

"And as Roosevelt drove by, he gave me the high sign, as if to thank me for respecting his wish," Joe said.

One other note regarding DiMaggio. I remember a conversation I had with him one time about when he played in Yankee Stadium when it was 457 feet to the left centerfield wall. We estimated that over a thirteen-year career, Joe probably hit 15 to 20 long fly balls each year that were caught that would be home runs today. So, instead of a total of 361 home runs, DiMaggio would have hit close to 600.

Joe said, "That's true, but don't forget I chased down a lot of shots in Yankee Stadium by other power hitters like Hank Greenberg and Jimmie Foxx that would have been home runs there as well."

Whitey and Yogi

Pitchers and catchers have an interesting relationship. They sometimes think alike, work in perfect harmony. Other times they argue without saying a word. Catcher wants a pitcher to throw something, pitcher wants to throw something else.

Pitcher wants to throw something, catcher wants something else.

Whitey Ford knew Yogi Berra pretty well and I asked him one time about having Berra behind the plate.

Whitey says, "Everybody thinks Yogi's a nice guy. Well . . . I was pitching against the White Sox and Yogi's catching. First batter, Luis Aparicio. First pitch, base hit. Next guy up is Nellie Fox. First pitch, base hit. That's two pitches, two hits. Next guy up is Minnie Minoso. I hit him by accident. Three pitches, three men on.

"Now Ted Kluszewski's up. I want to go with my slow curve to fool him. But Yogi always hated my slow curve, hated it. Yogi shakes me off. I'm calling for a slow curve and he's shaking me off.

"So I throw it anyway. Boom! Grand slam home run. Four pitches, four runs. And here comes Yogi, trotting out to the mound.

"I figure he's going to tell me, 'It's OK, it's the first inning, we'll get 'em back, don't worry.'

"Yogi looks at me and says, 'Whitey, take that slow curve and shove it up your ass.' "

The Pine Tar Game

I was there, at the replayed game, August 18, 1983. It was practically unannounced. There were more players and concessionaires than there were fans. There was no one there.

The umpires come out to pick up where they left off twenty-five days before, on July 24. They've announced that George Brett's ninth-inning home run, which was originally disallowed because Brett had too much pine tar on his bat, now counts.

The score goes from 4–3 Yankees to 5–4 Kansas City. Before the first Kansas City batter gets in the box, Billy Martin goes out on the field and goes to each umpire, claiming Brett and the base runner, U. L. Washington—it was a two-run homer—didn't touch all the bases. His contention was, how would they know since they weren't that original crew?

Typical Billy. Always trying to be one step ahead of the next guy. But it didn't help him this time.

The crew chief pulls out a piece of paper attesting to the fact that both runners touched each base, and the paper was signed by the crew that worked the disputed game. It was as if they had known Martin would pull something and, well, covered all the bases.

By the way, everyone has seen the TV replays over the years of Brett charging out of the dugout like an enraged bull, heading for Tim McClelland, the umpire who had called him out for the pine tar on July 24. Well, last year I asked Brett if he really would have physically attacked McClelland if he had not been held back by another ump, Joe Brinkman. "Are you kidding?" Brett replied. "No way! The guy was six-six, weighed two hundred and fifty pounds—and he still had my bat in his hands!"

Brett continued: "If you notice carefully, I made sure I stopped when I reached the umpires and began dancing around him [McClelland], just before Brinkman put the stranglehold on me. I couldn't beat up anyone, Warner. I couldn't even beat up you!"

Cy-Anara

This always sets me off: a pitcher winning the MVP.

I think that's wrong. A pitcher has his own award, the Cy Young Award.

An everyday player can't win the Cy Young Award, so a pitcher shouldn't be eligible for the MVP. You have to play awfully good ball every fourth or fifth day to be an MVP. Can you really be better than a guy who's out there 162 times?

This has happened before. It'll probably happen again. Doesn't make it right.

Bob Turley

I used to have a place on Marco Island in Florida and Turley had a house across the street. I ran into him one day, he says, "C'mon over, I want to show you something."

In his house, on the wall, he has every ball from the last out of every game he ever won. You point at a ball, he says, "Oh yeah, the Tigers, beat 'em 13–1." I point to one, I say, "What's this?" He says, "Nineteen fifty-nine, I almost had a no-hitter. I had two outs in the ninth against the Senators at Yankee Stadium, a game we won 7–0."

I say, "Who broke it up?"

He says, "Julio Becquer hits a little fly ball to left field and Norm Siebern plays it on the hop as if the score is tied. Didn't dive. He may have been able to make the catch. I struck out the next batter and that was it.

"I go in the clubhouse and there's Siebern sitting on a stool, crying. I never in my life had seen a player cry. I went over to him and he says, 'I should have gone for the catch. I'm sorry, Bob, I wasn't thinking. I may have caught it.' "

It took Hollywood nearly thirty-five years to capture that idea in a movie. Remember *A League of Their Own*, about women's baseball during World War II? Sure you do. Tom Hanks utters the line every kid knows by heart: "There's no crying in baseball."

I guess he was wrong!

Now Pitching

Talked to Bobby Thomson not that long ago. He's amazed that fifty years later people are still talking about that home run he hit to beat the Dodgers in the '51 playoff. Here's the part that amazes him.

He stepped out of the box while the Giants sent in Clint Hartung to pinch-run for Don Mueller, stepped out and was talking to himself. Said he never did that before. And he never noticed that Don Newcombe was out and Ralph Branca had come in to pitch. He was talking to himself, trying to get focused, and when he finally looked out there, it wasn't Newcombe.

Now, there wasn't any videotape then, just the radio. And that famous call, Russ Hodges' famous call on radio, was recorded by a Dodgers fan in his basement. He sent it to the Giants.

The announcer who did the play-by-play, who called Thomson's shot on national TV, was the great Ernie Harwell, the longtime Tigers announcer. And if that game was played today, it would be Harwell's TV call that would be remembered, not Russ Hodges' "The Giants win the pennant, the Giants win the pennant."

What, exactly, were Harwell's lost words?

Says Harwell: "Nobody remembers, except my wife. Only my wife heard the call."

Just for the record, Red Barber, the Dodgers announcer on radio, called it this way: "A high fly to left field, it's a home run. The Giants have won the pennant. Now a word from Schaefer Beer."

48

THE SPLENDID SPLINTER

If there was anything about hitting that Ted Williams didn't know, it didn't need to be known. To me, another mark of his greatness was that he could teach almost anybody the fine points of swinging a bat.

I remember one time at spring training with the Washington Senators in March of 1969, when Williams was managing the club. Everybody was standing around and Ted wanted to make a point to a player about hitting. So he took off his jacket and had a coach pitch to him.

It was amazing. Here he was, fifty years old, and he was banging line drives off the right field wall. That's some way to make your point.

Williams was a great batting instructor, no question. In that '69 season, he took a terrible team and finished fourth in the American League East, just one game out of third behind the Red Sox. Williams got every player to hit over his head.

Right fielder Hank Allen, Richie Allen's brother, was a .241 lifetime hitter who hit 36 points better (.277). The center fielder, Del Unser, who later played for Cleveland, the Phillies, the Mets and Expos, hit .230 in 1968. With Williams' help he batted .286. Ken McMullen, who played third base and had come over from the Dodgers, was a .248 lifetime hitter. In Williams' first year, McMullen hit .272, with 19 home runs and 87 RBI.

First baseman Mike Epstein, whom the Senators got from Baltimore and who had been a fullback at the University of California, was a .244 lifetime hitter. With Williams guiding him, Epstein hit .278, with 30 home runs and drove in 85 runs.

Ted helped left fielder Frank Howard, a huge and powerful man, be more selective at the plate and cut down on his strikeouts. Howard hit .296, with 48 home runs and 111 RBI. And shortstop Eddie Brinkman, who later went to the Tigers, had hit only .187 before Williams came along. In 1969 Brinkman upped his average 79 points and finished at .266. It was an incredible job Williams did.

You'd have thought that Williams, who retired as a player after the 1960 season, would have managed the Red Sox. He had been asked repeatedly by Red Sox owner Tom Yawkey to manage the team and Williams always gave the same answer: "No. Who needs that headache?"

But in 1969, Senators owner Bob Short offered something that Yawkey did not. If Williams would manage, Short would give him a stock option to buy 10 percent of the team. Williams, always an astute businessman, accepted the deal.

I remember asking him about being the last guy to hit .400, which is now fifty-nine years ago. And he said, "I think I would have had a good shot at it again in 1950. I had a great first half of the season but broke my arm in the All-Star Game at Comiskey Park, crashing into the wall while catching Ralph Kiner's long fly ball."

That led to surgery.

"After the operation," he told me, "my arm was never the same as far as getting the old snap back into my swing."

Williams, by the way, continued in that All-Star Game with a broken arm and even got an RBI single.

All I could think of was that he said his arm was never the same, yet he hit .388 in 1957 at age thirty-nine and won another batting title.

What if his arm had felt good?

After the final road trip of the '69 season, I took the plane back to Washington with the team and said to Ted, "You know what? You ought to quit right now."

He laughed and said, "Why?"

"Because you'll never get these guys to hit like this again."

He laughed again. Ted liked you if you weren't afraid to speak up. I guess because he always said his piece as a player.

THE VOICE OF THE FAN

Back when I used to sit in the bleachers at Griffith Stadium, the White Sox had an outfielder named Jungle Jim Rivera. Pretty good hitter and outfielder.

We're sitting there watching the Sox and Senators play one day and Camilo Pascual strikes out Rivera for the last out of the inning. Gets him with a slow curve. Jungle comes running out toward left field with his head down.

We're really giving it to him. Typical bleacher bums—long before the Cubs made the term famous.

"You really looked bad, Jim. You really looked bad. You missed that curve by twenty feet."

Rivera pauses, looks up and says, "I never could hit well against a last-place team."

What a comeback. We were finished—last-place fans.

MEDICAL MARVEL

Nowadays an injured player can take part in a game a couple of days after having surgery. Look at Randall Cunningham in '98 with the Vikings. Has his knee scoped Monday, practices on Wednesday, plays on Sunday. Wasn't always like that. Guys got hurt, they missed time, they didn't heal right, and they had to find a way to compensate. Unless fate took a hand. That's what I want to tell you about now.

It's 1953. The Senators were trailing the Yankees 22–1 at Griffith Stadium and the Yankees' Gus Triandos hit this ball against the center field fence. The Senators' center fielder, the late Jim Busby, was running full speed and he made the catch and crashed against the wall. He crumpled to the ground and he had to come out of the game.

I remember reading in the paper the next day that Casey Stengel said Busby was the kind of guy he wanted playing for him, losing 22–1 and he's still going all out to make a great catch. Well, about five years ago I saw Busby at a Washington Senators card show and I brought up that catch and he told me this story about how that injury actually saved his career.

Nobody knew it, he said, but he had hurt his right arm, his throwing arm, in the White Sox' minor league system, playing for Houston (Triple A). And because of that, he always played a pretty shallow center field. The reason, it turned out, was that he couldn't throw. But he kept his arm problems pretty much a secret. The shortstop and the second baseman would run out for the relays when he had to go deep into center, would help him compensate for the bad shoulder.

So he makes this catch against Gus Triandos and he leaves the game. They take him to the hospital and the Senators' trainer, Doc Lentz, tells him after they take the X rays that he could be out a month, just rest his arm over the weekend.

Monday they took X rays again and Doc Lentz stared at them with this shocked look. He tells Busby, "Try and move your arm in a throwing motion." Busby says, "What? Are you crazy?" Then he did it.

It was the first time in nearly five years he could move his shoulder. What happened? When he crashed into the wall, he ripped apart all the scar tissue that had formed when he was hurt in the minor leagues. For five years he couldn't throw the ball and now he was free to throw. And he was able to throw the ball the last nine years of his career.

For Busby, wall's well that ends well.

51

BILLY BALL

Off and on the field, nobody had been as active a Yankee as Billy Martin: player, manager, scout and front office.

Martin had been employed by the Yankees on a periodic basis for almost forty years. So who was better qualified than he to give an opinion on an all-time Yankee All-Star team? Here now, according to Billy and given to me by him in 1985, is Billy Martin's All-Time Yankee All-Star team of players he either managed or played with.

At first base, keeping in mind that Lou Gehrig was long gone when Martin came up, was Don Mattingly. Just one guy. No contest. A natural hitter and a Gold Glove fielder. Mattingly could always give you the long ball or the base hit, but almost always the RBI in the clutch.

At second base, Martin passed up his longtime second baseman, Willie Randolph, and chose a former teammate, Gil McDougald. He went with McDougald because Gil, who also played shortstop and third base, was one of the most valuable, versatile players Martin ever saw and he had to have a spot for him in the Yankee infield.

At shortstop, only one guy. A guy with whom he had played in all those World Series—Phil Rizzuto. Martin always pointed out that the only year he roomed with Rizzuto, 1950, was the only year Rizzuto was named American League MVP. So how bad an influence could Billy have been?

At third base, Martin said he would have to pick two guys, Clete Boyer and Graig Nettles. Except for Nettles being more of a power hitter than Boyer, he said there wasn't much difference between the two. He said both Nettles and Boyer were the finest fielders of all the Yankee third basemen he had ever played with or managed.

In left field, Martin picked Rickey Henderson. That surprised me a bit since, up to '85, Henderson had played for Martin only one year in New York, although he did have those great years for Martin when he was managing the A's. According to Billy, Henderson was one of the greatest offensive players in the history of the game—average, power and could steal bases, setting the record with 130 steals in 1982.

In center field, Martin went with Mantle. Although he saw Joe DiMaggio's last two years (1950 and 1951), he wasn't there for DiMaggio's great years in the 1930s and 1940s. For Martin, Mantle may have been the greatest Yankee of all time. There was nothing Mantle couldn't do, and with bad knees too.

In right field, he passed over Dave Winfield, who had super-years for Martin, and went with his old teammate Hank Bauer. Martin's description of Bauer: "Awesome, just awesome."

The catcher? Who else but Yogi Berra? As Martin pointed out, not only was Yogi a great hitter and a good defensive catcher, but he was "a mastermind behind the plate, calling the game." Martin said Yogi was "a brilliant tactician and never got enough credit for that."

Starting pitcher, left-handed: Whitey Ford. Who could argue? Ford was one of the great money pitchers in the history of baseball. "If you had to win one game," Billy told me, "Whitey Ford was your man."

For a right-handed starter, he had to pick two: Vic Raschi and Catfish Hunter. Martin said Raschi was the greatest competitor he ever saw as a pitcher and never missed a turn. Catfish, he said, never gave excuses. Martin said Catfish was the most honest player he had ever had. "When Catfish made a bad pitch, he admitted it and he took the blame."

Right-handed relief: not Goose Gossage, but Allie Reynolds. A starter most of his career, Reynolds became practically unhittable in the later stages of his career as a reliever.

Left-handed relief pitcher: Joe Page. For a few innings, when he was in his prime, Martin said, there was no one better than Page coming out of the bullpen.

I have always felt it was better psychologically for guys like Reynolds and Page in those days because there was no golf cart or car to carry them in from the bullpen to the mound. They had to walk. I can still see Reynolds jumping over the bullpen rail and walking toward the mound. It was like a boxer walking down the aisle, heading for the ring. I think the delivery cart took away one of the most colorful, dramatic sequences of the game, killed the sense of anticipation. I'm glad they finally did away with it for good.

Finally, Martin's all-time pinch hitter (and he had seen a lot of them): Johnny Mize, who was with the Yankees from 1950 to 1953. "Distance meant nothing to Mize," Martin told me. "If the fence was 350, Mize hit it 351. If the fence was 375, Mize hit it 376."

Pretty good team, huh?

I had known Billy for about fifteen years, first meeting him when he managed the Yankees in 1976 and I was doing *Monday Night Baseball* with Bob Uecker and Bob Prince on the ABC network. After a Yankees–Red Sox game at Fenway, won by the Yankees, Billy went back to the hotel with Uecker and me in the ABC limo. Billy was a good friend of Uecker's. On the way, Billy said he got so mad at George Steinbrenner for calling him up during the game that he ripped the dugout phone out of the wall. They had some relationship, with George hiring and firing Billy five times.

Over the years, one particular meeting with Billy stands out in my mind.

First, back in 1979, my wife and I took my youngest daughter, Shayna, who was nine at the time, into Billy Martin's Western Shop on Madison Avenue and 69th Street in New York. After buying a pair of cowboy boots for me, Billy took us all downstairs, where he had hundreds of cowboy hats on the shelves. He said, "Shayna, pick out a hat. It's my present to you."

One time, Billy put together a charity dinner for a friend of his, whose daughter had been stricken with a debilitating disease. The dinner was at the Hilton, near the Meadowlands. The place was sold out.

To show you what a nice guy he could be, he went to every table at the dinner, shaking hands with every single person, and there were more than 250 people—about twenty-five tables of ten.

He just wanted to personally thank all the people for coming.

COUNTING PITCHES

One thing that bugs me is the pitch count. Most managers say, "That's it, he's thrown enough pitches" rather than, "What's the score?" What makes this number so magical?

Do you think Bob Gibson ever cared about a pitch count? Before Game 2 of the '98 Series, we asked El Duque (Orlando Hernandez) about a pitch count. He looked at us and said through an interpreter, "I pitched all over the world before I came to the Yankees in 1998. We never had a pitch count."

I remember talking to Bob Turley, the Cy Young Award winner in 1958. He said nobody kept track of the number of pitches. You wanted to throw a complete game. Number one, it meant you were giving the day off to your bullpen. And, number two, that was a great bargaining point in your favor at contract time, how many complete games you had. The problem is, today that's the way they teach it in the minor leagues, that you're out of the game when your number's up.

That's the way these starters are brought up. They've got it in their heads that they're not going nine. After six innings they start looking at the bullpen. Plus, the managers are overprotective of these guys, because the club has invested millions of dollars in 'em. No manager wants to be responsible for overworking one of these precious arms.

I'm supposed to view the game with a professional's detachment, but I'm a fan and I remember when I went to games strictly as a paying customer. We valued good pitching. Growing up in Washington, I started going to games at Griffith Stadium in the late 1940s and one of the great parts of the afternoon was when the starting pitcher would come to bat in the last half of the eighth and get a nice hand from the crowd. We knew this would in all probability be his last time at bat and our last chance to show our appreciation before he would take the mound in the ninth inning to go for his complete game.

You rarely see that anymore. Of course, you'll never see it in the American League because of the DH. And you won't see many complete games, either. Blame it on the pitch count.

In 1981 I sat with New York's best all-time centerfielders *(from left to right):* the Yankees' Mickey Mantle, Brooklyn's Duke Snider, and the Giants' Willie Mays. (COURTESY OF WCBS-TV)

Yogi Berra told me that the best place to be on a cold day is behind the plate. (COURTESY OF DAVID SPINDEL)

The second time around I didn't ask Dustin if he knew who I was.
(COURTESY OF CHARLIE SIMMONS)

President Ronald Reagan: "If I had stayed on as a sportscaster, I might be doing the Dodgers games today and Vin Scully might be President."
(OFFICIAL PHOTOGRAPH—THE WHITE HOUSE, WASHINGTON)

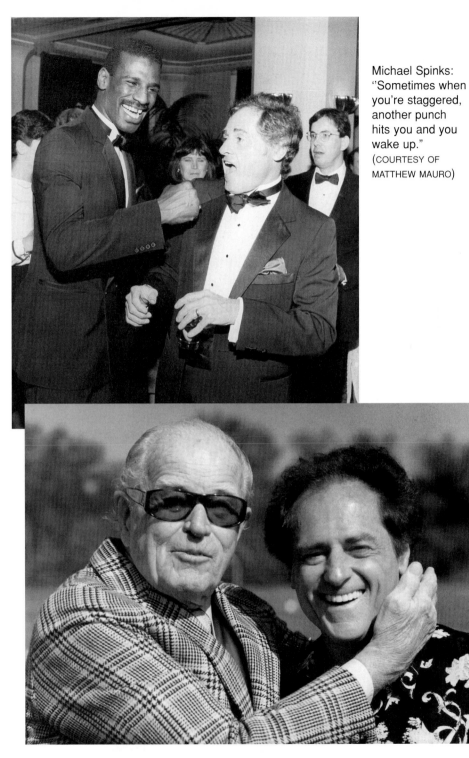

Michael Spinks: "Sometimes when you're staggered, another punch hits you and you wake up."
(COURTESY OF MATTHEW MAURO)

Jack Kent Cooke: "What happened to the horse race?"
(COURTESY OF THE WASHINGTON REDSKINS)

Muhammad Ali, 1998: "How come I stayed the same and you look older?"
(COURTESY OF RICARDO SANCHEZ)

Joe DiMaggio: "I would have hit at least 150 more." (COURTESY OF CARLOS ORTIZ)

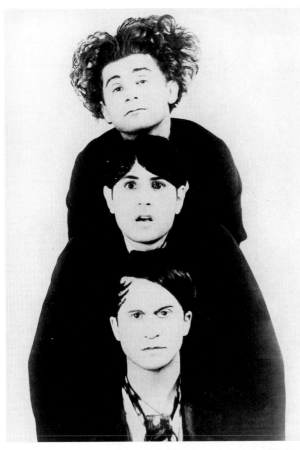

The Expansion Stooges, 1933 *(from top to bottom):* Mousie Garner, my father Jack Wolf, and Dick Hakins. (AUTHOR'S PERSONAL COLLECTION)

Joe Frazier: Muhammad Ali said he would make the heavy-weight champ the "first black satellite." (COURTESY OF WCBS-TV)

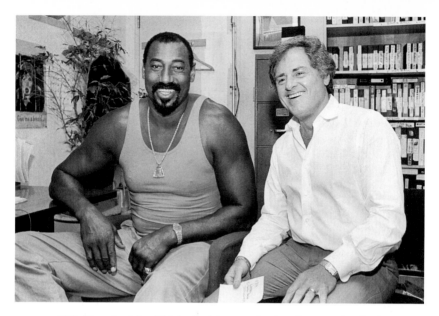

Wilt Chamberlain: "Triple doubles aren't what they used to be."
(COURTESY OF WCBS-TV)

Mickey Mantle: "Yogi had to jump so high, I couldn't see Larsen's last pitch in the perfect game." (COURTESY OF JUDIE BURSTEIN)

With cameraman Don Silverman at San Diego's Qualcomm Stadium right after the Yankees defeated the Padres in the final game of the 1998 World Series. I'm wearing a poncho to protect against a champagne dousing during the postgame interviews. (AUTHOR'S PERSONAL COLLECTION)

A shot of me in the press box area at Yankee Stadium. (AUTHOR'S PERSONAL COLLECTION)

Interviewing Shaquille O'Neal at Manhattan's All-Star Cafe (AUTHOR'S PERSONAL COLLECTION)

With Yankee skipper Joe Torre. (AUTHOR'S PERSONAL COLLECTION)

Hank Aaron: "I really hit 756." (AUTHOR'S PERSONAL COLLECTION)

THE CHEAP SAVE

Of all the useless, irrelevant numbers washing over us each day in a tidal wave of statistics in baseball today, nothing is as pointless as the save. Just show your face and you get a save. How bogus. It's meaningless.

Under today's guidelines, if your closer can't get at least 20 saves, then he doesn't belong in the majors.

Do you know what constitutes a save? If a pitcher finishes a game won by his team and he's not the winning pitcher, he gets a save if: he enters the game with a lead of up to three runs and pitches at least one inning; he enters with the tying run on base, at bat, or on deck; he pitches effectively for three innings.

If you retire a batter with the tying run on base, OK. You did your job. You should get the save. But to get a save because the guy on deck was the tying run, well, you gotta be kidding. The on-deck hitter may not even get up. How can you get a save against a batter you never faced? No good. Change the rule. Make a save worthwhile, meaningful.

You only get a save if you inherit the tying or potential winning run or runs already on base and you don't give up a hit, walk, a balk or hit a batter. You did your job. Game's over, and no one reached base through any fault of yours.

I think you should judge a relief pitcher by one criterion— did he allow the other team to tie the game? If he did, it's a minus. If he didn't, it's a plus.

Relief pitchers should also get minuses and plusses for other things. If you come in with two on and a two-run lead and give up a two-run double, that's a minus. Just because you're not charged with the runs because they were already on base should be no excuse. YOU let 'em score. You didn't do your job.

The scoring rule is one that they thankfully did away with—the game-winning RBI rule. Not the game-winning RBI that actually wins the game at the end but the RBI that put the team ahead so that they never trailed. In other words, if you drove in the run to break a 1–1 tie in the first inning and your team went on to win 10–9 and your team never trailed, you got the game-winning RBI. Not the guy who drove in the 10th run, which actually won the game.

Come on, gimme a break. What were these guys thinking? At least somebody finally woke up and changed the rule. But the point is, how could a so-called baseball official have instituted that rule in the first place? He could not have been brought up on baseball. But the rule did get changed so let's be generous. Let's award that giant of the industry a save for his meager efforts.

You want to hear another bad rule? If the Mets, Reds and Astros had finished the 1999 regular season in a three-way tie, the Reds and Astros would have played a 1-game play-off for the Central Division title, with the loser going home, and the Mets would have automatically been the wild card. Why? Because the Astros–Reds game would have counted as part of the regular season, which means the loser would have had a worse record than the Mets, being a game down in the losing column. You've got to be kidding! How unfair is that? If I was a Reds fan or an Astros fan and my team lost and I watched the Mets go into the postseason without even playing I would have gone crazy. Change the rule! Make it fair. In this case, the Mets should have to play the loser of the Reds–Astros game in a 1-game playoff with the winner becoming the wild card.

No way a team should just walk with a free ride.

54

FRANCHISE FREE AGENCY

My father took me to my first Senators game in 1947. A lot of those guys were bums but they were our bums. We felt like part of them and that they were part of us and it didn't matter how bad they were or how bad the team was. It was our bad team. There was a feeling of family, of belonging. It didn't matter if they won or lost—and they lost a lot—because you could root for your guys, your team.

That's been killed by two things—teams moving and free agency. They're the worst things that ever happened to sports. I don't know which is worse but my Washington roots tell me it's teams moving because it happened twice there. The original Senators left after the 1960 season and became the Minnesota Twins. That was a real knife in the back because, after all those years of being in last place, that team had Roy Sievers, Jim Lemon, Earl Battey, Harmon Killebrew, Pedro Ramos, Camilo Pascual, Zoilo Versailles, Jim Kaat. They were finally turning the franchise around.

No longer did we expect to lose. They were winning! They were finally getting over the hump. And they left.

If you were a baseball fan in Washington, and you had grown up with this team, that was devastating. Much like the Brooklyn Dodgers and New York baseball Giants fans. To a Washingtonian, this was just as criminal. Especially after Calvin Griffith said the Senators would never move.

Griffith, who had taken over the Senators from his father, Clark, who died in 1955, and who passed away himself recently, was notorious for not spending the big bucks on anything, not even his players. One of those players from the late 1950s, who was making $12,000 a year, told me Griffith was so cheap that in 1959, on a team flight from Washington to New York to play the Yankees, since lunch was served aboard the plane Griffith subtracted $3 meal money allowance from each player—and the meal allowance was only $10 anyway, which left $7 for dinner in New York. Talk about big spenders! Calvin, who was a twelve-year-old batboy for the Senators in 1924, the only year they won the World Series, was not one of them.

And what made it worse was the Twins went to the World Series in 1965. That was our team, or should have been, and they hadn't been to the Series since 1933.

If anything lessened the blow a little, it was that they brought in an expansion team in 1961. Called 'em the Senators. I know for myself I tried to get excited but it just wasn't the same. They were horrible and you couldn't love them the same way.

Then, in 1969, Ted Williams becomes the manager of the Senators. I'm working in radio by this time and it's a very exciting time because Vince Lombardi had just come over to coach the Redskins so we had two legends. Whoa!

After the 1971 season the Senators left again and moved to Texas. We lost two teams. It was a wrenching experience, just heartbreaking. Twice. Two teams.

I know about free enterprise and all that business, a guy has a right to make money off his team, but I'm telling you, as a fan it was every bit of miserable.

It's the same with free agency. As I said, the owners had it one-sided all those years—you know, "Sign this or we'll trade you to the St. Louis Browns." Who wanted to go to the Browns?

Now it's like "rent a player for a year and win a pennant." It killed one of the great things in baseball.

You could root for your guy. You knew he was going to be on your team forever, barring a trade. And you learned to love these guys. Mickey Vernon won two batting championships (in 1946 and 1953), played first base. He was a Washington Senator and he was our guy, although he did go to Cleveland in between. When Albie Pearson was rookie of the year, the fans loved him, all 5-foot-6 of him. He was a Washington Senator. He was our guy. Eddie Yost played third base for fourteen years.

When you went to the park, you knew Eddie Yost was going to be at third base, leading off. You would go and get a scorecard and the starting lineup would already be printed in it.

Today, the scorecard is simply blank.

MISNOMERS

Watching a baseball game the other day, the announcer says, "It's a home run, it hit the foul pole."

How can it be the foul pole if it's a fair ball? It can't be the foul pole if it's a fair ball. Either call it the fair pole or make it a foul ball but you can't call it a foul pole if it's a fair ball.

Same thing with the foul line. Can't be the foul line. Ball hits the line, it's fair. Call it the fair line.

I don't know where these things come from. I don't know why they bother me. But there they are and they bother me. Baseball should rename them.

Same thing in football. You've got an offensive tackle, he can't tackle anyone. If he does, it's a penalty.

A safety? You get tackled in your own end zone and give up two points. What's safe about that? That should be called a setback.

And why is the fullback in front of the halfback? Shouldn't

he be fully back, all the way back, behind the guy who's only halfway back?

Then there's free agency. Nothing free about it. Sign a player and he's expensive. Let's call it expensive agency. And the next guy who says he would play the game for the love of it should be made to do exactly that.

One more. The prevent defense. Have to say it right— Preeee-Vent. Prevents nothing. The only thing the prevent defense does is it prevents you from winning the game.

CLICHÉS

Are you tired of hearing the same old repeated baloney, the same old clichés, coming from players and coaches before and after games and at press conferences?

Let's stop it now. Why can't there be a little creative thought, a little clever chatter, something more than the boring and banal and, worst of all, the bland?

Know what I'd like to hear from a professional athlete who signs a multiyear contract with a huge bonus? I'd like to see the guy stand up and say, "Forget that other crap. I did it for the money. Period! The money was the big reason." You've got all these players who love to talk about playing for the love of the game and saying it's not about the money. Until they get offered a contract for less than they think they're worth. OK, admit it. It is about the money.

And when did 110 percent become the standard? What happened, 100 percent is no longer sufficient? Did it get hit by inflation? One hundred percent is good enough for me.

Then you have the players and managers and coaches who always say, no matter how many games they're behind, that "We only take it one game at a time." That's no good anymore. I want to hear one of them say they're going to take it two games at a time.

That would be a good line from a "hard-nosed player." Where have all the soft noses gone?

And how about when a big-time Division 1-A college football coach, on the eve of playing a winless Division II opponent, tells us, "We can't be overconfident. They could surprise us." Tell the truth for once. The only surprise would be if the other team actually shows up. Say it—"This is a mismatch. They don't have a chance. Get 'em out."

Well, that's enough on this topic. I've got to put my pants on one leg at a time, put on my sportscasting face and take it one broadcast at a time.

And I promise to give it 110 percent.

57

THE ARTHUR MERCANTE STORY, OR HERE'S THUMBS IN YOUR EYE

Ali is fighting Frazier in their first fight, March 8, 1971, which I thought was the greatest fight of all time. It's the only one where the heavyweight champion and the former champion are undefeated. Neither Frazier nor Ali had lost a fight and the former champion, Ali, is undefeated because of his special situation. Years later, I'm interviewing Hall of Fame referee Arthur Mercante and he tells me about something that happened in the ninth round that night.

Ali and Frazier are in a clinch, he goes to separate them, and accidentally sticks his thumb in Frazier's eye. Frazier starts yelling, "I can't see, I can't see." In Frazier's corner, Yank Durham is yelling, Hey, give us time. And Mercante's trying to think what to do. Mercante, one of the greatest referees of all time, is thinking the fans are going to go crazy, and who ever got thumbed by a referee? So he says, "C'mon guys, keep fighting." Fortunately, it was near the end of the round and Frazier got a minute to recover, got his vision back and the fight went on.

You know, I always loved boxing. First sport I ever followed. I used to listen to the Friday night fights with my father. We used to sit there and watch the radio and score the fights. Really. We looked at the radio, just the way you look at the TV. Hey, it's where the sound came from and it captured our attention. When things got really exciting, you moved closer to the radio as if you were trying to stick your head into the middle of the action. Don Dunphy called the fights and he was the greatest.

My father used to buy me *Ring* magazine and I memorized it. I was seven years old, and I loved it. That's how I got interested in sports. A lot of people tell you stories about their father coming home from the steel mill and throwing a ball with them but this is how I got into sports. My father took me to these arenas around Washington, all of them gone now, and we watched the fights. Everybody goes nuts for heavyweights but that was the time of the middleweights—LaMotta, Graziano, Zale. But there were great fighters in each division, even featherweights—Willie Pep.

That's what's killing boxing today. Then you had only one champion in each division, eight champions. You didn't have these fake divisions, strawweight, cruiserweight, these fifty-one alphabet champions. It was totally different. You knew who the fighters were. I didn't go to a baseball game until I was ten—just wasn't interested. But I became interested, in that and football. Boxing, football and baseball. Those were my three sports.

Ali, on the Air

Had Ali on my radio show one night in Washington in 1968. That's the kind of thing you want to tell everyone is going to happen but there's always doubt he'll show up so I never announced he was coming on. And sure enough, around 8:30, here he comes, with a small entourage. And we talked for an hour. He was the greatest salesman I've ever seen.

But you know what was funny? Nowadays you'd have PR people faxing everybody everywhere to tell 'em about your big coup—an interview with Ali. A whole hour! We've got him. But then? I wasn't even sure he'd show up. Today you'd be pushing it for ratings, worrying just as much about who heard you as what you said. If there were ratings in those days, nobody knew about them. I certainly didn't. Nobody said, Gee, you sure had a big audience last night. The show just went on. If there were ratings, no one was aware of them. I'm sure they had a way of knowing if you were doing your job or if you were going bad. You would know—they would take you off the air.

And the night we had Ali on, we talked boxing for about an hour. We didn't talk politics. It's hard to believe but we treated sports as sports. He talked a little about his beliefs but we mostly talked about fights and fighters and it was one of the first times he did this great little poem about Joe Frazier.

It went like this:

> *Now Ali lands with a right*
> *What a beautiful swing*
> *But the punch lifts Frazier clear out of the ring*
> *Frazier's still risin'*

But the referee wears a frown
'Cause he can't start countin'
Till Frazier comes down
Now Frazier disappears from view
The crowd is getting frantic
Our radar stations have picked him up
He's somewhere over the Atlantic
Who would have thought
When they came to the fight
That they'd witness the launching
Of a black satellite?

Now, I interviewed Ali many times over the years since our first meeting on that radio show in 1968. The last time I interviewed him Ali was here in New York in 1999. After the interview, I said, "Champ, I've known you now for over thirty years." He looks at me, bends down and whispers in my ear, "How come you look so much older and I stayed the same?"

Protect Yourself at All Times

Talked to former heavyweight champion Jack Sharkey one time, the only man to fight both Joe Louis and Jack Dempsey. The only man. So Sharkey fights Dempsey in 1927 for the right to fight Tunney, after Dempsey lost to Tunney in 1926.

So Sharkey and Dempsey fight in July of '27 and the winner's going to fight Tunney in September. In that fight, Dempsey hits Sharkey with a low blow and Sharkey turns to complain to the referee and boom! Dempsey hits him and knocks Sharkey out with a right hand to get the rematch.

So I'm talking to Sharkey and he's about eighty years old. He says, "You know, I got $225,000 from that fight in 1927. I built a mansion in New Hampshire with that money and I still live in that house."

That's protecting yourself.

Now I'm a guy who loves TV but I can't apologize for the bad things that came out of it. And TV ruined the fight game. There weren't enough fighters to feed the medium so you had fighters who didn't have enough experience being pushed onto TV. From Friday night fights to Monday, Tuesday and Wednesday night fights, and it killed the small arenas. People said, "I'm not going, I'm going to watch it on TV." And the places where these guys learned their craft dried up.

I asked Jake LaMotta what he thought about all these guys getting title shots so early, Leon Spinks getting his shot at Muhammad Ali in his eighth professional fight. LaMotta didn't get a title shot until he'd been fighting eight years.

He said, "I wouldn't have been ready. I would have been afraid to get a title shot after seven fights. Those other guys were too good." He waited because that was the way you did it, you had to learn the craft.

There were more, better fighters and that's it. That's really it. If you ask most people . . . go on the street and ask people, excluding Roy Jones Jr. and Oscar De La Hoya, name me the top fighters. They can't do it.

Mike Tyson's a sad case. No footwork whatsoever. He's fought only two guys who had good left jabs—Buster Douglas, who knocked him out in the tenth round in Tokyo in

1990, and Evander Holyfield, who knocked him out in the eleventh round in 1996 in Las Vegas.

Drive, He Said

I got in a cab one time in Miami. The driver says, "What do you do for a living?" I say, "Sportscaster." He says, "Sportscaster? You ought to know who I am. I used to be a fighter."

I don't know. He's an older, white-haired guy. I don't know. I say, "What weight?" He says, "Light heavyweight."

I look at him again, I say, "You aren't Joey Maxim, are you?" He says, "Yeah."

I said, "You fought Sugar Ray Robinson in 1952 for the light heavyweight title. Robinson was way ahead and collapsed in the fourteenth round because of the heat."

Maxim looks at me in his rearview mirror and says, "Yeah, and I had air conditioning in my corner."

The Straight Truth

Evander Holyfield was in New York to fight Henry Akinwande in the spring of 1998.

Akinwande was supposedly the number one contender. So I say to Evander at the press conference, "If you hadn't been ordered to fight this guy, would you sign for this fight?"

He says, "No, I wouldn't take this fight." And Akinwande is standing right there. I thought that was great. Holy Moses, an honest answer. Most people would have told us what a good fighter Akinwande was and how he deserved a shot at the title. Not Holyfield. In his opinion, the fight was a waste of time.

All I could think of was in this day and age of pro fight ballyhoo and fake fights at press conferences to help promote the gate, here's Holyfield telling us the truth—that the fight was not worth our while. Well, as fate would have it, the fight never did come off: Akinwande had to pull out because of hepatitis.

DECISIONS, DECISIONS

When Evander Holyfield and Lennox Lewis fought to a supposed draw in their first fight in March of '99, the cries of "highway robbery" quickly filled the air and the newspapers. Some people even called it the worst decision of the decade, giving boxing a black eye and the sport a bad name.

Boxing is beyond that and will survive. Besides, how can you give boxing a bad name?

What bothers me is the politicians who jump on the bandwagon and want to hold investigations. What grandstanders. Bad as it was, the Holyfield–Lewis decision was no worse than some of the calls in the NFL especially during that '98 season—like Jerry Rice's nonfumble in the 49ers–Packers wild card game. Remember? Rice fumbles, the whistle blows, suddenly it's no fumble and the Packers wind up losing. Or when Vinny Testaverde scored the phantom touchdown against Seattle, even though he was down at the one? Where were those mass-hysteria politicians then? Why no investigations?

Boxing, with its sordid history, gets no points for good behavior.

There wasn't one positive thing that came out of Holyfield–Lewis. Holyfield was terrible. He looked like the picture of Dorian Gray, aging suddenly in the ring as we looked on. Lewis could have finished him but showed no killer instinct. Too cautious. The fight was there for him to take and he didn't take it. That's why the scoring was close.

The judge who took the most heat was Eugenia Williams who had it 115–113 for Holyfield. Well, she really only made one huge mistake. Giving Holyfield the fifth round 10–9 when it should have been the other way around, 10–9 for Lewis. But even if she had scored that round properly, her card would have read 114–114, almost the same as the 115–115 on the English judge's card. So it's still a draw–a majority draw. One fighter cannot win when two of the three judges score it a draw.

And the judge who scored the fight 116–113 for Lewis only gave him one more point than the guy who had it 115–115. That's what happens when every round is scored either 10–9 or 10–10. You're only going to get a 10–8 round when there's a knockdown or a totally lopsided round where one guy does everything but go down. That's why the scoring can be close.

Bad as this was, it was not the worst decision I've ever seen. The Shannon Briggs–George Foreman fight in 1997, won by Briggs, was far more unfair. And if you want to go back a little ways, the first Joe Louis–Jersey Joe Walcott fight in 1947, in which Walcott knocked Louis down twice and lost a split decision, was certainly very poor. Louis thought he had lost and left the ring before the official announcement was made!

Both of those were worse than the Holyfield–Lewis draw but they all point to the same issue: The average fight fan does not know what goes into scoring a fight.

Look, there are no touchdowns or home runs in boxing. It's strictly human judging.

Again, as bad as this was, it was no worse than some of the judging we've seen in Olympic figure skating, and you never saw a politician jump up and down over that, did you?

Fights are supposed to be judged on four categories: clean punching, effective aggressiveness, ring generalship and defense. Punches should hit the target areas crisply, the fighter should be moving forward and pressing the issue, he should be using the ring and appropriate tactics and he should be blocking and slipping punches.

Each category should count 25 percent. But as longtime boxing judge Harold Lederman told me, that's usually not the way it works.

"If you hurt the other guy with constant clean punching throughout the fight, thoroughly beating him, that will be 95 percent, leaving only 5 percent for the other three categories," he said.

Another big misconception is this. You always hear an announcer say, "This guy landed three times as many punches as that guy." Well, that doesn't mean beans. It's the quality, not the quantity. If one guy lands fewer punches but his are more effective, then he gets the point. You are not paid by the punch.

So the next time you score a fight at home, maybe you'll have a better insight into what's going on in the minds of the judges.

DON'T BE LIKE MIKE

Yeah, I know he was the youngest heavyweight champion ever. Give him credit for that. But I think most of the heavyweight champions down the line would have beaten Mike Tyson. And I'm beginning with Jack Johnson and I'm not skipping a whole lot of guys.

Jack Dempsey, Gene Tunney, Max Baer, Max Schmeling, Joe Louis, Rocky Marciano, Jersey Joe Walcott, Ezzard Charles, Sonny Liston, Muhammad Ali, Joe Frazier and Larry Holmes (at his peak, and because of his great left jab) would have beaten Tyson.

As the years pass, boxing will forget Tyson, except for his biting of Holyfield's ear and that his self-destructive nature made him his own worst enemy. The fighter who really defeated Tyson was Tyson.

I also have this to say to the court in Montgomery County, Maryland, that sentenced Tyson to one year in jail for punching and kicking two older men after a car accident—

good for the judge. Just because Mike Tyson is Mike Tyson, he should not have made the sentence any lighter. You beat up a sixty-three-year-old man and a fifty-year-old man and you should receive at least a year in jail.

Life didn't treat Mike Tyson well when he was growing up but he had a second chance, a third chance, a fourth chance. His toughest opponent was never the one in the ring, always the one in the mirror.

HEAD GAMES

For years, people have proposed headgear for boxers during their actual fights, the same protective gear they wear in training with their sparring partners. One night in New York, I asked a couple of top boxers about that suggestion.

We had gotten together at a private showing of a Sugar Ray Robinson special produced by HBO and I put the question to welterweight champion Oscar De La Hoya, light heavyweight champion Roy Jones Jr., lightweight champ Shane Mosley and heavyweight contender Michael Grant. To a man, they all said headgear would be no good during bouts.

De La Hoya told me it would hurt his ability to avoid the heavy blows to the head.

"In training it's difficult to slip punches because of the extra padding around your head," he said. "You think you are slipping the punches by an inch but the punches will still land because of the headgear. You can't see the punches coming from the left side, the right side or even the uppercuts. You actually want to get rid of the headgear in training."

Jones put it another way: "Guys take more punishment in the gym than they do in the ring. Even with the headgear. That's where the wars are, where you get caught more."

Mosley said the headgear "stops you from getting cut but it doesn't stop brain damage."

Grant, the heavyweight, took another approach. He told me, "It wouldn't be boxing if you had headgear. That's what separates the amateurs from the professionals."

Even before interviewing these fighters, I had heard from Angelo Dundee and other fighters that Muhammad Ali took much more punishment in training with his sparring partners, who tried to tear his head off and make a name for themselves, than he ever did in the ring.

Talking to Michael Spinks one time, he pointed out that being knocked down and knocked out were the only things you couldn't practice and prepare for in boxing. Spinks, remember, was undefeated until Mike Tyson KO'd him in a minute and a half of the first round of their title fight in Atlantic City.

Spinks also said that what people didn't realize was that sometimes after taking a punch on the chin and being staggered, another punch on the chin could actually clear your head. It would sort of wake you up and help you focus your attention on what was going on.

Of course, it didn't seem to help him in the Tyson fight.

GENTLEMEN, START YOUR ENGINES—
I DON'T THINK SO!

If any sport turns me off, it's auto racing. Never interested in it. I don't care how fast a guy can go. Jim Murray had that great line about "gentlemen, start your coffins" and Dick Young called it "coffins on wheels." With all respect to the drivers, they do risk their lives, have great stamina and concentration and mistakes could be deadly. But are they athletes?

If you take the greatest driver in the world, say Jeff Gordon, and you give him a bad car, he's not going to win the race. Not going to win the race. Take a lesser driver and give him the best car, he's going to win the race. If there's a machine involved, are you an athlete? Where's the sport in it?

And this always bothers me. There are more deaths in auto racing than in boxing, even with the intent in boxing to injure. There's no intent to injure in auto racing but even the fans get killed. In boxing, you hit one guy and he gets hurt. In auto racing, you hit one guy and he gets hurt, two other guys get hurt, tires go flying and some expensive machines get torn to bits, with pieces occasionally getting into the stands.

Whenever I hear these congressmen saying they want to ban boxing, I say, Why don't you look at auto racing? Neither one should be banned but, bottom line, there's a big lobby for auto racing—sponsored by auto companies, tire companies, tobacco. Who supports boxing? Nobody. That's a double standard. Don't give me that stuff.

62

BALLPARK BLUES

These days, it seems that the first thing any self-respecting team owner does is demand a new ballpark that looks like an old ballpark. But does he put the kind of name on it that resonates with history? No! He sells it to the highest bidder.

Sorry, it all seems plastic and antiseptic, too clean and too corporate. If I'm going to Washington for a game, I'd like to be at the Capital Centre. I can't warm up to the MCI Center or other places with phone-y names: ALLTEL Stadium in Jacksonville, Qualcomm Stadium in San Diego, which used to be Jack Murphy Stadium, named after the sportswriter who helped bring baseball to town.

The airlines have Continental Airlines Arena in East Rutherford, New Jersey, the Delta Center in Salt Lake, the United Center in Chicago, the Trans World Dome in St. Louis.

You've got your RCA Dome in Indianapolis, your Compaq Center in Houston, your FleetCenter in Boston. ARCO

Arena in Sacramento. Tropicana Field in Tampa. The Molson Centre—what, no Montreal Forum anymore?

In the 2000 season alone, four baseball teams will begin playing in new stadiums: The Astros are going to Enron Field, the Brewers to Miller Park, the Giants to Pacific Bell Park, and the Tigers to Comerica Park.

If you ask an average sports fan today where these places are, he can't tell you. And if you ask that fan to name the top three famous sports ballparks, the list would include Wrigley Field, Fenway Park and Yankee Stadium. Although a new Fenway Park is being built, they're history and they're still standing.

Twenty-five years from now, a ten-year-old budding sports fan is going to ask his father, "Dad, what was Yankee Stadium?"

And just what might we be calling Yankee Stadium? Maybe "The House That George Sold."

DINING OUT

There's probably nothing more outdated than the lyrics to "Take Me Out to the Ballgame." Buy me some peanuts and Cracker Jacks? I'm not sure if anybody does that anymore when they head for the concession stands or wave to a passing vendor while taking in the spectator sport of their choice.

I have been to almost every ballpark in the United States, beginning with Griffith Stadium in Washington, D.C. It was a ballpark, not a mess hall. Hot dogs, peanuts, popcorn, Cokes, beer and ice cream. Six items! That was it.

Today there are over sixty items in some parks. You ever go to Camden Yards in Baltimore? Besides the regular ballpark chow, they even have their own deli. Wander out to right field and you're at Boog's Barbecue, named for its beefy proprietor, former Orioles first baseman Boog Powell.

Some people go to eat in the restaurant at the ballpark and watch the game on TV monitors. I've never understood that. You could stay home and eat and watch the game on TV, plus at home your parking is free, there's no wait at the rest room and you beat the crowd.

There's no end to what you'll find on the menu now. They even have sushi bars at ballparks. How about a fish taco in San Diego? A Dodger Dog—a monster hot dog for two people. Fajitas. There is no end. You can even warm up with hard liquor or have champagne and wine with your exotic meal.

Give me a hot dog any day. Especially at Fenway Park. Of all the hot dogs I have ever had at a ballpark—normal size dogs and grilled well done, please—none were better than the ones served on the top of the roof at Fenway. It probably sounds funny to say that one hot dog sticks in your memory, but the one I had on the roof that late night in May of 1970 before I broadcast a Senators–Red Sox game does for me.

A hot dog just goes with a baseball game but you need some variety in your diet. Second best for me were the crab cakes in the press room at old Memorial Stadium in Baltimore.

The best beer after a game? In the Bard Room at old Comiskey Park in Chicago.

Best peanuts—the ones sold outside Griffith Stadium by one particular vendor, a Filipino who had only one eye. He bagged the peanuts himself in a brown bag, wound tightly at the top. Nobody ever bought peanuts inside the stadium. We all bought from him. We were told years later that the guy sold so many 25 cent bags over his long career that he became a millionaire, retired and went to Florida.

There was an art to the way the ballpark vendors would serve their hot dogs in those days. They carried them around in a big iron container strapped over their shoulders. When you were in the stadium and ordered a dog, the guy would whip out the dog, tear the paper it was wrapped in, take a wooden slab and slap on the mustard. If you were a few rows back, he would then rewrap the paper and throw the dog (now coated with mustard) up to you and you would toss the money back at him—35 cents.

As I grew older, we used to sit in the Beer Garden, an extension of the left field bleachers that faced the field at Griffith Stadium. We used to stand up, hold up our beers and yell at the batter to hit one in our cup. We would yell at Harmon Killebrew, the future Hall of Famer, who was fifth all-time with 573 home runs, "Come on, Harmon, hit one in our cup."

No one ever did.

Summer of 1956. As usual, first-place Yanks versus last-place Senators. But it didn't matter. They were our last-place Senators. The great Whitey Ford pitching for the Yankees, who would go on to win another World Series, while the Senators would go home.

Well, on this one particular night, who was at the game, sitting in a box behind first base? President Eisenhower, who was a frequent unannounced visitor to Griffith Stadium.

The first time up against Ford, Senators outfielder Jim Lemon (who would later manage the expansion Senators) hits a home run. The second time up against Ford, Lemon hits another home run. The fans are going crazy!

Lemon's third time up—Boom!—another home run. Three times at bat against Whitey Ford and three home runs! In fact, the last two homers were caught by the same guy in the Beer Garden.

So, with the Senators trailing 5–4 in the last of the eighth, Lemon comes up for the fourth time to face Ford. With the fans giving Lemon a standing ovation as he approaches the plate, Casey Stengel comes out and takes Ford out of the game. Tom Morgan comes in and strikes out Lemon—but there's another standing ovation as Lemon heads for the dugout!

To this day, it's the only time I ever saw a standing ovation given to a batter who had struck out.

WHAT'S IN A NAME?

Nicknames have always been part of American life—not only in sports but in all fields. Tricky Dick Nixon, Scarface Al Capone, William "Billy the Kid" Bonney, General Black Jack Pershing, Martha Jane Cannary (come on, you've heard of Calamity Jane).

It's an affectionate tag (usually) we put on people, as if we're saying we know the person, we're insiders.

It's of course a standing part of the sports fan's life—to be able to refer to favorites by something other than their given names.

Two-Ton Tony Galento (who actually weighed 233 pounds and stood 5-9 when he knocked Joe Louis down before losing to him). Smokin' Joe Frazier. Archie Moore, the Old Mongoose.

Wilt the Stilt. Sleepy Floyd. Marvin "Bad News" Barnes, all from basketball. Can you imagine going around your whole life being called Bad News?

Boy, if you liked nicknames then you loved the old Los Angeles Rams of the 1950s. Skeets Quinlin, whose real name was Volney. Elroy "Crazy Legs" Hirsch. Does that name paint a picture? Vitamin T. Smith, whose real name was Verda Thomas Smith. No wonder he used a nickname. And then there was the 6-3, 225-pound Paul Younger, known as Tank, at fullback. (Today, of course, on some teams "Tank" would be the smallest guy in the backfield.)

They competed in an era where there should have been a Super Bowl of nicknames. The Colts had Eugene "Big Daddy" Lipscomb and a center named Madison "Buzz" Nutter.

Go back a little further and you find Ace Clarence Parker, Bullet Bill Dudley and Byron Raymond "Whizzer" White, who became even more famous as a Supreme Court justice.

Now sometimes, unfortunately, one single play can almost overshadow a career and hang a moniker on a player forever. Roy Riegels, who ran a fumble toward his own goal line for California in the 1929 Rose Bowl, is always referred to as Wrong Way Riegels. The Vikings' Jim Marshall did the same thing against the 49ers just up the coast at Kezar Stadium in 1964. The all-timer is probably Giants first baseman Fred Merkle, who cost the team the 1908 National League pennant with a critical omission. Merkle was on first base but neglected to touch second on what should have been a game-winning RBI single. The run was nullified, and the Giants lost the pennant in a one-game playoff against the Cubs. From that day on the play was known as Merkle's Boner and he is forever remembered as Bonehead Merkle.

Baseball, which has the longest history, also had the most

nicknames. And the coolest ones. You could go back to the turn of the century (the last century, folks, not this one) and find Charles "Piano Legs" Hickman in the outfield. I'm not sure if he ever met another outfielder, James "Bug" Holliday. Bug? Who wants to be called Bug?

I guess it beats Pig, as in Frank "Pig" House, a Tigers catcher in the '50s. And Joseph Michael Medwick was just Ducky. You could pair him with Goose Goslin. But keep them away from James "Hippo" Vaughn. And there was an obscure pitcher in the 1880s named William Van Winkle Wolf, who was known as Chicken. Chicken Wolf? No wonder he never won a game. We could throw in Bill "Moose" Skowron but that's a little misleading. He got that name as a kid and it had nothing to do with any shaggy beast of the great north woods. He had a shaved head and a friend called him Mussolini, after the Italian dictator. It got shortened to Moose.

But if you want a big animal, one that's at home in New York, I guess you settle on King Kong—Charlie "King Kong" Keller of the Yankees.

When Keller was in the outfield, he was usually joined by Joltin' Joe DiMaggio, the Yankee Clipper, and Tommy Henrich, known as Old Reliable. I'd rather be any of those than Puddin' Head, as in Willie "Puddin' Head" Jones of the Phillies.

Some of the tags hung on players came from their physical features or even disabilities. There was William "Dummy" Hoy, who played fourteen years in the majors, from 1888 to 1902. Why was he called Dummy? Because he was deaf. As a result of his inability to hear, umpires began using hand signals at the plate for a strike, raising their right hand. Before, the calls were verbal. But Hoy, of course, couldn't hear them. Hence the ump's flying right hand, which we still see today. Ernie Lombardi, a catcher in the '30s and '40s, won two batting titles but what did they call him? The Schnozz. Come on, the guy was a terrific ballplayer and we honor his nose?

How about Frank "Home Run" Baker? Yep, he led the league in homers four times—with 11, 10, 12 and 9 (1911–1914).

There was Happy (Felsch), who unfortunately was thrown out of baseball in the 1919 Black Sox scandal and who was anything but happy. There was Stinky (Harry Davis), Swish (Bill Nicholson, who struck out a lot) and Stuffy (McInnis). Sounds like tryouts for the Seven Dwarfs.

OK, let me give you my favorite four baseball nicknames in descending order.

Batting fourth, the St. Louis Browns outfielder (1917 to 1926)—William Chester "Baby Doll" Jacobson. You can't be called Baby Doll and play in the major leagues. Maybe you should be in *A League of Their Own.*

Batting third: George "Twinkletoes" Selkirk. Excellent hitting outfielder for the Yankees in the '30s and '40s.

Batting second and catching: Bubbles Hargrave. He played for the Reds and Cubs in the teens and '20s and then for the Yankees in 1930. Born Eugene Franklin Hargrave. Every time Bubbles unstrapped his chest protector and shed his shin guards his teammates yelled, "Take it off."

Batting first and pitching: David Meadow Ferriss. He pitched for the Red Sox from 1945 to 1950, career record 65-30, shut out the Cardinals on a 6-hitter, 4–0, in Game 3 of the '46 World Series. The nickname strapped to this 6-2, 210-pound right-hander: Boo! Boo Ferriss. Not Bo. Boo.

They'd be cheering but they're BOO-ing. Sounds like an invitation to the fans—Boo Ferriss.

Ya gotta love him. He would have to be my all-time Boo of the Week.

THE EYE OF THE BEHOLDER

You know how we were talking about picking one pitcher to win a game or one running back to gain the toughest yard? Well, that's the key to sports being so much fun. Discussions, arguments, passionate ranting, all of it based on personal observations and regional loyalties.

I think I'll start another argument. What's the most exciting home run in baseball history? And, while we're at it, the most exciting touchdown and the greatest shot in basketball history? The answer is the same for each one: It's strictly subjective.

I guarantee you, if you're from Pittsburgh, then Bill Mazeroski's home run to end the 1960 World Series rates at the top. If you're from New York, it's Bobby Thomson's HR against the Dodgers in the final 1951 playoff game (did somebody say Bucky Dent against the Red Sox in '78?). How about the Blue Jays' Joe Carter's home run against the

Phillies? It all depends on where you are from and who you were rooting for.

Same for the touchdowns. Joe Montana to John Taylor to beat the Bengals in the '89 Super Bowl in the final minute? John Riggins' run against the Dolphins in Super Bowl XVII? Alan Ameche's overtime TD against the Giants for the 1958 NFL title? There's no right or wrong. No one will convince you and you will change no one's mind.

What's the greatest college basketball game of all time? Was it North Carolina's 54–53 win over Kansas in triple overtime for the 1957 championship? Christian Laettner's shot to beat Connecticut? N.C. State's 1974 103–100 overtime win against Maryland for the ACC title? Take your pick, folks. I'm sure if you went to Texas Western (now Texas–El Paso), it's the Miners' win over Kentucky in the 1966 NCAA final.

Greatest fights? Where do you start? How about 1971, Ali–Frazier, the first fight, when both guys were unbeaten? Dempsey–Tunney, with the long count. The second Louis–Schmeling fight, with Louis knocking out Schmeling in the first round. The three Zale–Graziano fights. Hagler–Hearns. The first Duran–Leonard fight.

OK, now that you're good and riled up, I'm going to give you my picks for the best of the best. And I'll be honest— they're based on my age and who I was rooting for at the time.

Home run: Bobby Thomson. I saw it on TV when I was nearly fourteen and watched it with a friend of mine from Brooklyn, Bobby Lipman. He went crazy, threw his school books on my floor, slammed the door and went home.

Basketball game: George Washington vs. West Virginia, in February of 1957. Uline Arena, in Washington. The place held 5,000 fans. GW had no big-name players. West Virginia, a huge favorite, had Hot Rod Hundley. GW led most of the game but tried to slow the ball down toward the end (this was the era before the shot clock). West Virginia tied the game, it went into overtime and West Virginia finally won it 113–107.

Best fight: Ali–Frazier. Fifteen rounds of great action. Frazier knocks Ali down with a left hook in the final round and wins the decision.

Best all-around fighter: Sugar Ray Robinson. Great boxer, outstanding footwork, could knock you out with either hand.

Best single round of boxing: 1985, first round of Hagler–Hearns.

Feel free to argue among yourselves.

FORECLOSURE

The hardest thing to do in all of sports is hitting a baseball. Hardest thing to do in sports. Don't let people tell you that it's harder to hit a golf ball. One is stationary and one is coming at you at 90 miles an hour. You're trying to hit a round ball with a round bat.

Also: Baseball players play golf on their day off and play pretty well. How many golfers play baseball on their day off?

67

POSTER BOYS

Do athletes owe it to society to be role models? Are they role models? Should they be?

I can tell you that, growing up as a teenager in the 1950s, I never had one athlete as a role model. And the guys I grew up with felt the same. It was important to us to follow a path and the lessons that our parents laid down for us. After a game was over, we never even thought about a ballplayer or tried to be like him.

We didn't take the guy home with us in our minds. We discussed the game and a player's performance on the field but that was it. We may have tried to emulate a player in our sandlot games but that meant copying his batting stance, not his personal morals. We didn't go to bed thinking, Gee, I want to be like this guy or that guy. Our parents laid down the rules and that was it. Those were the guidelines.

If you didn't follow them, you got punished. But that was

fair and it was part of the risk you took if you knew you were doing something wrong.

Being a great ballplayer doesn't make someone necessarily a great person. The only thing a player owes to society is to conduct himself as he (or she) would even if he wasn't a big-name athlete. He should be treated no better or no worse than your everyday person who isn't a ballplayer. To say the athlete owes it to society to be a good citizen because he is a role model to youngsters is not right. He owes it to society because those are the rules for everyone.

I agree with Charles Barkley on this. He should not be responsible for being a role model to children. Whoever is responsible for bringing up a child should be more of a role model to the child than Charles Barkley. When you get right down to it, Charles is only a basketball player. What about when his playing days are over? He's out of the picture and not a role model anymore because he's not playing and youngsters have now moved on and picked another role model who is still shooting and rebounding and dribbling.

Sorry. No good. It's like saying this movie actor or that rock star or this doctor or that lawyer is my role model. Chances are, those people you want to idolize don't know you, don't know you're alive. And the only way you think you know him is by what you read or hear or watch on TV. It has nothing to do with what the person is really like.

Now you can admire somebody or enjoy their work—but that's it. It's not that person's responsibility to be your role model.

Hey, I used to like Bugs Bunny cartoons when I was growing up.

But that being said, he wasn't a role model.

PETE ROSE

Should Pete Rose be in the Hall of Fame? Yes!

Why? Because even if he did bet on baseball—and that has never been proven in court—it's been eleven years since he was suspended from the game.

Ironically, two nights before Bart Giamatti's famous news conference on August 24, 1989, baseball asked Rose if he would accept an eleven-year ban and then be reinstated. Rose said no. If he had agreed, he would have been eligible for reinstatement this year and would eventually be inducted into the Hall.

Rose has paid his dues. He has served his penalty.

Look at Steve Howe or Darryl Strawberry: How many chances did they get? Over and over for drugs and booze, and each time baseball let 'em back. I didn't see Strawberry or Howe sitting out eleven years.

When Paul Hornung and Alex Karras were suspended for

gambling on their teams in 1963, did they have to sit out eleven years? No—just one season.

I say Rose has served his time. Enough is enough.

Reinstate him this year.

For youngsters to continue going to Cooperstown and be cheated out of any reference to Rose is a crime.

DOPE IS FOR DOPES

Are sports teams and leagues too lenient when it comes to penalizing players for using drugs? YES!

Bottom line, it could ruin the game. Will fans continue to go to games if they think players are on drugs and not giving their best performance? I don't think so. The current rules are too lax. A player is given too many chances to come back. So apparently, to the players, drug use is worth the risk.

The problem is that the player is protected by the players union. But is the union helping or hurting the player?

My proposal: Every player who signs a professional contract must also sign a separate piece of paper. He signs it in front of his attorney, his parents, his wife and his children. The paper is separate from his contract and clearly states: "From this day on, if I am caught using or distributing drugs, I fully understand that I will first be suspended for one season without pay. If there is a second violation, I will forfeit the balance of my salary and I will be barred from this sport for life."

He then signs another line below that which states: "I fully understand the above statement and accept the consequences." His lawyer, his parents, his wife and possibly children also sign under the athlete's name.

Number one, most everybody in life, depending on the severity of the crime, deserves a second chance. That's why, though the penalty is harsh for the first offense, it is not career-ending. But it should be harsh enough to make the individual think hard about doing it again.

Why the big production about the player's family being present and producing their signatures? Because it is a family venture. No matter how you look at it, any violation of the contract affects not only the player but his entire family. Perhaps the thought of a player's family and his attorney, who may also be a close friend, being present upon the signing will mean something extra as far as the commitment goes.

The other reason for the tough penalty? Hopefully it will help the junior high or high school or college student who is now gearing himself up for pro ball. If he knows now that he only gets one shot in pro ball, instead of two or in some cases three, maybe it will help him fight temptation along the way. In the NBA they finally instituted penalties for using marijuana. First violation: counseling. Second violation: five-game suspension and $15,000 fine. Big deal! In a sport where the average salary is over $2.5 million, $15,000 is chump change! And what's a five-game suspension? In an 82-game schedule, that's nothing.

Now, you may say my proposal won't change anything. Well, you may be right. But one thing's for sure: It sure as heck isn't working the way it is now.

OLYMPIC GOLD, BROUGHT TO
YOU BY . . .

I first covered the Olympics in 1976 for ABC network TV and I have to tell you it was a special kind of thrill. That was the Winter Games in February in Innsbruck, Austria, and the memorable Summer Games in Montreal in August. It was great just being there but broadcasting some of the events really put it over the top for me. You don't often walk around in awe of your surroundings but it's pretty hard not to be dazzled by the Olympics, with athletes and fans from every part of the world converging for this spectacle.

I remember walking down the street with race car driver Jackie Stewart in Innsbruck. He was like a king. Everyone stopped him and asked him for his autograph.

My specialty was the speed skating events in Innsbruck. I

remember Sheila Young of the U.S. winning gold and Dorothy Hamill grabbing everyone's heart in figure skating.

The Summer Games were terrific, especially boxing. The U.S. had just an outstanding team, with Michael and Leon Spinks and Sugar Ray Leonard. Everybody was up, everybody was loose and it was beautiful.

Today it's another story. Sure, there was some commercialism then, but not like now. It has gotten so big and with the TV rights fees soaring out of sight, they should probably call the Olympics the Corporate World Sponsorship Games. Too much.

Everything is the official something of the Olympics—the official drink, the official car, the official watch, the official shoe, the official pen. I wouldn't be surprised if the officials are the official officials. Enough.

Whatever innocence was left in the Games is gone. As soon as someone wins the giant slalom, he's waiting for a professional contract or signs with a sponsor at the bottom of the hill. And some of the events—come on! The old standards still hold up well—skiing, skating, boxing, basketball, track and field, ice hockey. But what is synchronized swimming? C'mon, give me a break. These things just take up space, fill the oversold airtime.

And now, instead of putting a premium on the Olympics and making them a spotlight event once every four years, they alternate the thing on a two-year rotation—winter, summer. More is not better. But it does put more money in the International Olympic Committee's pocket.

Too bad we can't turn Ken Starr loose on the IOC. He could help us get through all the dirt the guardians of the Games heaped on themselves in 1998.

It all started when an IOC senior member, Marc Hodler

of Switzerland, accused Salt Lake City and other Olympic cities of participating in vote-buying schemes. A Salt Lake official admitted spending $400,000 on scholarships and athletic training for thirteen people, which included six relatives of IOC members, and the scandal spread. You know the old argument—everybody does it. And apparently everybody did it. Cities paid bribes, IOC voters took them gladly and then asked for more. Gifts, scholarships, jobs for their kids, you name it and they did it.

And sitting atop this mound is Juan Antonio Samaranch, the Olympic dictator, acting as if he'd never heard that this goes on. And he's the one who appoints the IOC members. This isn't sport. It's politics. Clean it up, clean 'em out.

But this taint runs through too much of the Olympics and some of it won't ever be fixed. One of the compelling stories in the 1972 and '76 Olympics was the dominance of the East German women swimmers. We have found out since, of course, that they were given steroids, that they were chemically enhanced. This is a nice way of saying they cheated.

Some of the German doctors who gave the swimmers these male growth hormones were eventually sent to prison or fined. But were the swimmers forced to give up their medals? No! The IOC rejected the U.S. swim team petition to take away the medals and award them to the legitimate competitors. The IOC said it would create legal problems.

Why? Just scratch all the guilty East German swimmers who received medals and move up every other swimmer who finished behind one of them. For example, if a U.S. swimmer finished second to a guilty East German, disqualify the East German and award the gold to the U.S. swimmer. I'm not suggesting the IOC just take away medals any old time, but there is a precedent. Jim Thorpe had the two track and field medals he'd won at the 1912 Games in Stockholm, Sweden, taken away because he had previously played minor league baseball and was therefore considered a "professional"—which is ironic, because nowadays you can be a professional and still compete in the Olympic Games. By the way, Thorpe's amateur status was restored in 1982 and the medals returned to his family in a speical ceremony during the 1984 Games in Los Angeles.

The Olympics are supposed to provide a great opportunity to meet in friendly competition and shake hands, not grease palms.

71

NO WAY, NCAA

When will the NCAA finally get it? We want a national champion in major college football. Why is that so hard to understand?

They have hockey playoffs, basketball playoffs, baseball playoffs, soccer playoffs, lacrosse playoffs, football playoffs at levels below Division I-A. But somehow they can't figure out how to run a championship for the big boys.

What is this Bowl Championship System? Come on. That's practically a test for which school has the best math department, figuring out this rating and that schedule and multiplying by nine and adding three unless it's Wednesday. No one can figure this out. It shouldn't be that hard, either. Do the uncommon thing—use common sense.

You pick the best eight teams, any way you want. Then the winner of the Rose Bowl plays the winner of the Sugar Bowl. The winner of the Fiesta Bowl plays the winner of the Orange Bowl. The following week (use the NFL bye week before the Super Bowl, if there is one), you have the two winners meet for the NCAA Division I-A football championship. Three weeks. That's it. And it's over.

I think it's wrong to use the writers' poll or the coaches' poll to decide who plays where at the end of a season. With coaches, it's certainly a conflict of interest. How can a coach objectively decide where another coach and his team are going to play? Same thing with the writers. They have to write for somebody, somewhere. Aren't they going to be partial to a team they write about on a daily basis or a team in their area? No good.

I say we leave it up to a committee of noncoaches, non-writers. Forget the bogus polls and let this committee, composed of Division II administrators and commissioners, who are not involved in any way in this playoff, decide who participates in the tournament, creating each bowl matchup.

Although it worked out perfectly this past season, with Virginia Tech playing Florida State, the two best teams in the country, normally that's not the case. For example, here's the way I'd have seen the '99 bowls working out and leading up to a national championship.

The winner of the Fiesta Bowl, which matched Florida State (11-1) and Tennessee (12-0), would have played the winner of the Orange Bowl game between Syracuse (8-3) and Florida (9-2) in one semifinal. The Sugar Bowl winner of Ohio State (10-1) and Texas A&M (11-2) would have met the Rose Bowl winner of Wisconsin (10-1) vs. UCLA (10-1) in the other semifinal.

The two survivors would play for the title in the week off before the Super Bowl.

Only two teams would play all three weeks and four

teams would be done after one week. Four teams would play just twice.

When it's done, you have an NCAA champion. It might not be perfect, but you can understand it. Or were you fascinated by another Insight.com Bowl matchup?

72

HOOP-LA

I don't care who wins the NCAA college basketball tournament. I didn't go to any of the schools in the tournament (I graduated from American University and AU never, ever makes it), I don't personally know any of the coaches or players on the teams and I don't bet on the games and don't play in an office pool. So who cares who wins?

Unless a New York team is in the tournament, I don't root for anyone. I do think some of the games are fun to watch, especially if the team has had an exciting season, but who wants to see Duke beat Lenoir Rhyne by 56 points in the first round, or watch Kentucky clobber Catawba by 60 in the second round? What's the point of watching, unless you went to Duke or Kentucky or you're in the office pool or you bet the game?

The only thing I root for is a fast game, so that our late newscast doesn't come on at 12:30 or one o'clock in the morning.

Plus, there are too many teams in the tournament. Sixty-four teams? Come on. Some of the teams shouldn't be in there. Put a premium on the qualification to get in. Eliminate some of these first- and second-round blowouts.

But that's what TV wants, so that's what TV gets. Programming, lots of it. To show you how things have changed, let me take you back to 1966. I and another longtime Washington broadcaster, Dan Daniels, did the Final Four and championship game from Cole Field House on the campus of the University of Maryland for WTOP radio. There was no national TV and there were still tickets available the day of the games.

And yes, that's the year Texas Western upset Kentucky.

I don't think WTOP paid over $200 for the rights to broadcast that game.

The championship game, which started at 8:00 P.M., was over by ten minutes to ten. I left Cole Field House on the Maryland campus, drove home and was in by 10:30. The game was no big deal then. Certainly not like it is today.

73

TOLL BOOTHS, SHOOTING ONE

You know how the average person drops a coin at a toll booth. Out comes the arm, flips the coin, off they go. Well, what about a guy like Shaquille O'Neal?

Do you think Shaq just drops his money in a toll booth, or does he slam it?

Do you think Patrick Ewing goes through a toll and ever wants to get out of his car, sneak up on someone else dropping their money in and swat it away before it goes through the basket?

Or does Michael Jordan want to get out of his car, move back two car lengths and try for a three-pointer?

This is what sitting in traffic on the 59th Street bridge will do to you.

74

THE LARGE APPLE

One thing you have to remember in New York is that the sports fans know as much or more about what's going on than you do. So you have to keep on top of things. Number two, you never talk down to the New York audience. Always treat them as your equal. That probably goes for all cities but especially in New York, where the fans are so rabid and plugged in.

New York differs from other cities in that there's so much of everything and the fans follow all of it. Three hockey teams, two basketball, two baseball, two football and that's not even counting the colleges and the interest in college basketball. Fan loyalties are divided here—Mets fan, Yankees fan; Giants fan, Jets fan; Knicks fan, Nets fan. And there are the Rangers, Islanders, Devils fans.

In Washington, by contrast, there are no divided loyalties. Everyone's a Redskins fan, all year-round. That makes it a unique market too.

I think that's one of the things that gave me a problem when I went back to Washington. I've always tried to be objective and not be a homer. Now, I like the home teams to win, I root for them, and why not? It makes my job easier. But I would pick the Redskins to lose—on the air—if I thought they were going to lose.

In the three seasons I was on the air in Washington, the Redskins were 9-7 in 1992, 4-12 in '93 and 3-13 in '94. Coming off their Super Bowl win in January 1992, quarterback Mark Rypien was a holdout. He didn't look that good as a result, and in their first meeting of the regular season I picked the Cardinals to beat the Redskins, even though the Skins had beaten the Cards seven straight times. The phones began to ring and the letters came. I'll never forget this one letter: "Dear Mr. Wolf. Pick with your heart, not with your head."

Well, the Cardinals won the game 27–24, and it was like I had defamed somebody's relative. But I never had a problem with that. I always felt that was the way you should do it. I remember we did a Redskins show each Monday after the game. Redskins tight end Donnie Warren says to me (off the air), "I hear you picked us to lose." I said, "Yes, I did." I guess he wasn't used to hearing that.

We had two other sportscasters there at Channel 9—Frank Herzog and Ken Mease. And one game against the Dolphins, in 1994, we all went on the air and picked the Dolphins to win. I said, "This has to be the first time in the history of Washington sportscasting that three guys from the same station have picked the Redskins to lose." I'll guarantee you it was. And the Redskins did lose the game. It had to be extra tough for Frank to pick against the Skins because he was their play-by-play man.

I think in another city that would be appreciated because of the honesty and because you're analyzing the game. In Washington, that doesn't go. They'd rather see you pick the Redskins and be wrong, because then you're one of them.

In New York, it's different. Because the loyalties are so divided. Over the years I have picked either the Giants or Jets or both to lose the same week. And I've never received one complaint. Probably because when you pick the Giants to lose, you make the Jets fans happy. And when you pick the Jets to lose, you make the Giants fans happy.

You have to love New Yorkers. They're able to put aside their own happiness for the moment and enjoy someone else's misery.

TUNA TOWN

I have known Bill Parcells since he first took over the Giants in 1983. Let's establish one thing right off the bat: The man is a great coach. He gets the most out of his talent and can get players to perform over their heads.

Some people say he is pompous, rude, sarcastic or all three of the above. He may be. But I would rather listen to his press conferences than most of the babble that comes from the other coaches in the league. To a man, most of them are dull and say nothing except how great the team they're going to play is. Parcells cuts through all of that public relations baloney and just lays it on the line.

From a sportscaster's point of view, his sound bites are great. Whether he comes off surly or cruel or humorous doesn't matter. He is the master of the sound bite. He is not dull.

In his first press conference after coming back to coach the Jets in February of 1997, Parcells looks up and says to me,

"Welcome back, Warner. You came back, just like me." I said, "Yeah, package deal." I left to go to Washington the year after he left the Giants and I came back to New York February 3, 1997. He returned from New England to coach the Jets two weeks later.

At another press conference, after he benched his starting quarterback, Glenn Foley, in favor of Vinny Testaverde, he says, "I just saw a difference in Foley since he got hurt. I can't explain the difference to the average person. It just comes from experience." He says it's "like the difference between you"—and here he looks at one of the sportswriters—"and Dave Anderson." Anderson, of course, is the Pulitzer Prize–winning columnist for the *New York Times*. Then he says, "Or the difference between you"—and he looks at the sportscasters—"and Warner Wolf."

Now that was funny (at least for me) and a great sound bite. I ran it on my show and it got a big laugh in the studio.

The next week at Yankee Stadium, I ran into Dave Anderson. I said, "Dave, I'm in good company. I think Parcells is partial to the old guys."

I mentioned to Parcells at a press conference in January 1999 that we were witnessing sports history just before the Jets played the Broncos for the AFC championship, with him taking his third different losing team—Giants, Pats and Jets—to the conference championship or the Super Bowl. Lombardi, Landry and Halas won titles, but only with one team.

But Parcells said that was an unfair comparison because times have changed. He said football is like other businesses today. Owners want immediate success. There is practically no grace period, no time to build a program slowly. As a result, coaches, like other business executives, move on, even when they've had success. In Halas' day, and Lombardi's and Landry's, coaches stayed in one place, even though Lombardi did come back briefly with the Redskins. Dallas had only one coach for twenty-nine years but three of them since Landry was fired.

And Parcells is right. Look at Bart Starr. Nine years as head coach of the Packers, with a record of 52-76-3. No way he'd last nine years today, legend of Titletown or not. What about George Seifert? He won a whopping 76 percent of his games and took the 49ers to two Super Bowls and it wasn't good enough. So now he's coaching the Carolina Panthers. His final year with the 49ers: 12-4.

How about the five coaches fired in one day at the end of the '98 season? Five out of thirty, purged in one bloody day. No way that would have happened in the past. Parcells hit the nail squarely with his blunt hammer. This is the way it is now. No wonder coaches like Parcells, Jimmy Johnson in Miami, Mike Holmgren in Seattle, Mike Shanahan in Denver and Tom Coughlin in Jacksonville are also in effect the general manager and the coach. If you're the GM, you're not going to fire yourself!

It's the same thing in baseball. Look at ex-Indians manager Mike Hargrove. All he did was take Cleveland to 5 consecutive playoffs and 2 World Series. The result? He was fired because he didn't win the World Series. Can you imagine if John McGraw managed today? Managed the Giants for 31 years, won 10 pennants—but only 3 World Series. C'mon, get him out of there! Or how about Connie Mack, who owned and managed the Philadelphia A's for fifty years. He only won 9 pennants and 5 World Series. C'mon, no good, Connie! Fire yourself—you're holding up progress!

HALL OF FAME, OR HALL OF SHAME?

So Lawrence Taylor was inducted into the Pro Football Hall of Fame. Boy, what a debate that kicked off in January 1999 when he and four others were elected the day before Super Bowl XXXIII. The issue: character.

There has never been, nor will there ever be, a question about Taylor's ability on the field. He could dominate a game, make a team alter its game plan just to try to neutralize Taylor, or at least control him a little. But that wasn't the contentious question for the Hall of Fame voters. It was character.

His off-the-field conduct, which would make him a first ballot choice for the "Not a Model Citizen" Hall of Fame, left the voters with a problem. Hey, Taylor's record speaks for itself, including his suspension while playing for using drugs. Look at the facts: arrested for using and buying drugs, deadbeat dad, filing false tax returns. So how come Taylor or anyone else with such a deplorable history can make it into the Pro Football Hall of Fame?

Easy! Because, according to the Hall's voting criteria, the only thing that counts is what a player achieved on the field. What a bad message for the young future football players around the country! You can break the law, but as long as you are a great football player it doesn't matter. You will still be rewarded.

The point here is not to say that Lawrence Taylor doesn't deserve to be in the Hall of Fame. Under the NFL rules, he does—and it would have been an injustice if he didn't get in. But it's certainly time to review those bylaws.

Right now, if you have big problems off the field, the rules are Taylor-made.

77

MY MOST MEMORABLE
FOOTBALL GAME

New Year's Eve, December 31, 1972, the Redskins played the Cowboys for the NFC championship. Keep in mind the Redskins hadn't won any championship of any kind since 1945. And the Redskins were underdogs, even at home.

It was a four o'clock game and George Allen did something you could never get away with today. After the Cowboys had been introduced, George kept the Redskins in the locker room until 4:15. When the Redskins came out, the fans were in such a frenzy it was unbelievable. What a psych-job. Today the NFL controls every aspect of the game, but what a ploy by George Allen.

The score was 10–3 Redskins at the half and in the second half Billy Kilmer hit Charley Taylor for a touchdown that made it 17–3 and the Redskins won 26–3. Curt Knight kicked four field goals and the Redskins won the NFC championship and went on to the Super Bowl.

In the final minutes, the people began to realize how significant this was, the first championship in twenty-seven years, and the whole crowd at RFK began singing "Amen." You know, Aaaaay-men. It made me tingle. That was probably the most exciting, electric moment I've ever witnessed at a game. Of course at the time I was a Redskins fan. Even though I was a broadcaster I was a Redskins fan.

It's an injustice that George Allen is not in the Hall of Fame. He ought to be in. No question he was an innovator. He was the first to really develop special teams as a separate unit with their own coach. He even introduced the special teams once before a game, which you never see anymore, always offense and defense for television. He just wanted them to get some recognition.

Allen did some amazing things. One season he gets Bill Malinchak from the Detroit Lions and he announces that Malinchak will block a punt before the season is over. Well, they open the 1972 season with the Vikings on *Monday Night Football*. The Vikings had been 11-3 the year before, losing to Dallas in the NFC playoff. Sure enough, Malinchak blocks a punt, it goes for a touchdown, and the Redskins beat the Vikings.

George Allen thought of every angle. I really admired the guy. I know he didn't win any championships as the head man but he was also the defensive coach for the '63 Bears when they won the NFL title, holding the opposing teams to an average of less than two touchdowns per game. His winning percentage was close to .700.

But George could rub people the wrong way. Edward Bennett Williams once said, "I gave him an unlimited budget and he exceeded it." And when he got fired by the Rams, owner Dan Reeves said, "I had more fun losing." You know how George hated losing—as much as he hated the Cowboys. One time he gave a pep talk to the Redskins players before a Dallas game and he got so wound up he said, "I want to fight Tom Landry. Right now."

I asked George once why he hadn't taken Kilmer out of a game and put in Sonny Jurgensen after Kilmer had thrown seven consecutive incomplete passes. And George says, "Warner, there are no relief pitchers in football."

AMERICA'S TEAM

I'll admit it. I used to root against the Dallas Cowboys, wished desperately for them to lose. I couldn't help myself.

I saw the Cowboys through the eyes of a Redskins fan who grew up in Washington. I saw every Cowboys–Redskins game, either live or on TV, from the time Dallas came into the league in 1960 to the time I left Washington in 1976. It was a great rivalry, a bitter rivalry, especially after the Cowboys started to improve, finally playing Green Bay for the NFL championship in 1966 and '67.

I remember in the early 1960s when Tom Landry would rotate his quarterbacks on every down. Eddie LeBaron in, Don Meredith out. He didn't rotate them every drive or every quarter but every single play. LeBaron would be in on first down, Meredith second down, LeBaron third down. It would continue throughout the game. Can you imagine a coach trying to pull that now? The quarterback's agent would say play him or trade him but don't rotate him and the media would be all over everybody. It's a wonder the Cowboys ever won a game under that system. And of course they didn't in 1960, going 0-11-1, tying the Giants 31–31. LeBaron retired after the '63 season, Meredith became the number one QB and was later followed by, among others, Roger Staubach, Craig Morton, Danny White, Gary Hogeboom, Steve Pelluer, and Troy Aikman.

A Cowboys–Redskins game that always sticks in my mind was their meeting at RFK in 1965. Dallas jumped off to a 21–0 lead and still led 31–27 with less than a minute left. Sonny Jurgensen takes the Skins down the field and throws a touchdown pass to Angelo Coia, who appeared never to have complete control of the ball in the end zone before dropping it. The Cowboys complained bitterly to no avail and the Skins won 34–31.

Dallas turned that around on the Redskins in 1967. Jurgensen had put Washington ahead 14–10 late in the game but Meredith throws a pass to Dan Reeves (the one now coaching the Atlanta Falcons) coming out of the backfield. Reeves, running down the sideline, practically becomes invisible. He got by All-Pro linebacker Chris Hanburger, who was one of the last of the great small, fast linebackers in the NFL, and there he went, untouched by human hands, ghosting his way 70 yards for a touchdown and a 17–14 win. In one play after the Redskins went ahead, the Cowboys took it back and 55,000 fans went from mass hysteria to total silence. There was absolutely no sound during the 70 yards Reeves ran. It was as if it wasn't happening.

Of all the games, I think that's the one that started the intense rivalry, and George Allen, who arrived to coach the Redskins in 1971, fueled it even more.

Allen loved veterans and brought in players from other

teams who would make up the "Over the Hill Gang"—Ron McDole from Buffalo, Diron Talbert and Maxie Baughan from the Rams, Billy Kilmer from the Saints and later Kenny Houston from Houston. And don't forget Verlon Biggs, Roy Jefferson, Tommy Mason, Jack Pardee and Richie Petitbon. When the Skins beat the Cowboys 21–16 in Dallas in Allen's first season, they went to the playoffs for the first time since 1945.

And, as you know, in 1972 they beat Dallas in the NFC championship game on New Year's Eve in Washington and went to the Super Bowl.

And of course Dallas got even in 1974 on Thanksgiving Day. Every Redskins fan had his dinner ruined when Clint "The Mad Bomber" Longley came in for the injured Roger Staubach, hit Drew Pearson with a 50-yard bomb for a touchdown in the final minute and gave the Cowboys a 24–23 win. Longley later got in a fight with Staubach and got traded, which Redskins fans thought served him right.

Dallas knocked Washington out of a trip to the playoffs in 1979 when Staubach led them back from a 13-point deficit in the final two and a half minutes. The Cowboys, down 34–21, scored a TD, got the ball back with 39 seconds left, and Staubach hit Tony Hill. Rafael Septien kicked the extra point and Dallas won 35–34, another miracle in its pocket.

That's the kind of stuff the Cowboys did that made them so popular and that made them so easy to hate when they did it to your team.

When I moved to New York in 1976, it just wasn't the same. The Giants and Cowboys never developed the same sort of rivalry, one that you could feel in your bones. When the Cowboys played the Redskins, all of Washington knew it was Dallas Week. I don't think in Dallas anyone looked at the schedule, circled the date in New York and called it Giants Week. It was more like a vacation week. From 1974 to 1980, the Cowboys beat the Giants twelve straight times.

In New York that wasn't called Dallas Week. It was just another lost weekend.

79

THE DAY I SACKED THE REDSKINS QUARTERBACK

Eddie LeBaron was the Redskins quarterback in the mid-1950s. Wonderful player. They called him the Little General. He was 5-6 and a great ballhandler. In 1955 the Redskins with LeBaron finished 8-4-0—their best record till 1971, when George Allen came in and they finished 9-4-1. They were not very good in those losing years.

LeBaron, in the off-season, was going to the George Washington University law school and I was a student at GW then, undergraduate. This was February of 1956, two months after the Redskins' 8-4 season. I was playing intramural basketball. My fraternity was so good we had three teams—the A team, the B team and the C team, for Clowns. I was one of the Clowns.

Our first game was against the GW law school, and who plays for the GW law school? Eddie LeBaron. I was the same size as him, so I had to guard him. Me, guarding Eddie LeBaron.

Late in the game there's a loose ball that's near us and we both went for it and we collided. Boom, down we go. And everybody comes over, very concerned, and they're all asking Eddie LeBaron how he is. Nobody asked me.

All I could think was, "Oh, man, don't tell me I hurt the quarterback of the Washington Redskins." Everybody's helping him up, patting him, and I'm sprawled there, completely ignored.

Boy, was I glad he was OK, but it taught me an important lesson. If you're going to crash into someone, make sure he's less famous than you are.

OT

Worst rule in the NFL, most unfair rule, is the overtime rule. You flip a coin, I win the toss. I move 40 yards, I kick a field goal, game's over, you never touch the ball.

Can you imagine that in baseball? Yanks–Red Sox, tied 3–3 after nine. Red Sox bat in the tenth and score, game's over. No good. The Yankees never come to bat.

The dumbest argument is that the team that wins the toss only wins the game about half of the time on its first possession. Like that somehow makes it fair? That's a lame argument. That's half the time too often.

Both teams have to touch the ball. Steal the college rule if you have to, let 'em have four downs from the opponent's 25 until someone scores and the other team doesn't.

But this? Boo. Not right, not fair.

THE KNEEL DEAL

Whiat's the worst part of an NFL game? The end, if it's a blowout and the quarterback is taking a knee.

What is more useless or boring in the entire world of sports than watching a quarterback take a step back and place his knee on a lawn of fake turf? Come on, give me a break! My grandmother could take a snap and kneel on the ground!

Change the rule. In the last two minutes of the game, with a 21-point lead or more, you have to hand the ball off. There has to be an exchange of the ball between the quarterback and another player. You know that a ball carrier is not going to just stop and fall down once he gets the ball. At least give the fans their money's worth. Nobody pays to see a quarterback kneel down with the ball.

It would be like a baseball game where, with two outs in the top of the ninth and the home team ahead by 10 runs with no one on base, the winning pitcher doesn't have to throw the ball to the last batter. He can just kneel down on the mound. Who needs the third out?

Hey, you can't kneel down in basketball with a 20-point lead and 30 seconds left so you can watch the clock run out. No good. And a boxer who's way ahead on points in the last round can't look up at the clock, see that there's only five seconds left and take a knee to preserve the win. People would boo and say he took a dive.

I don't want to see another quarterback kneel down. Unless his name is Neil Downe.

BROWN POWER

I always felt Jim Brown was the greatest runner of all time and I still do. You know what bothers him?

They play 16 games and they still put all this emphasis on gaining 1,000 yards.

A thousand yards? That's 65 yards a game. Brown told me he'd be ashamed if he only gained 65 yards a game. That's ridiculous. He says if you play 16 games, you had BETTER gain 1,000 yards.

He's amazed football hasn't raised its criteria, and he's 100 percent correct. The 1,600-yard-season should be the baseline for measuring excellence in running backs. A thousand? C'mon, that's yesterday's news.

I interviewed Brown last January and we talked about why he left the game when he still had so much left. He said he retired at age twenty-nine because after nine years in the league he had accomplished everything he wanted. He didn't want to be like other players he saw, hanging around two or three years too long, their skills heading downhill. I asked him if he was ever tempted to come back or if anyone ever made an effort to have him un-retire.

He said Art Modell, the owner of the Browns (who held his rights in retirement), sent L.A. Rams owner Carroll Rosenbloom to Europe to see him. They wanted to know if Brown, then filming *The Dirty Dozen,* would be interested in coming out of retirement if the Browns traded him to the Rams, where he would be close to Hollywood. Brown said that once he turned down that deal, that was it. Everyone knew he was serious about staying out of the game.

I also asked Brown if he thought it was true that he was a better lacrosse player than football player.

"Well," he said, "you have to remember I had played lacrosse since grade school in Manhasset, Long Island, and was a lot bigger than most of the other midfielders."

All I could think of was the sight of Jim Brown running downfield with a stick in his hand.

Except for lacrosse fans, most people don't know much about the sport or about what Jim Brown did in that area, but he was one of the greatest high school and college lacrosse players ever. His legacy is in football.

When Barry Sanders' father says Brown remains the measuring stick, the greatest running back in history, he's absolutely right. Currency is based on the gold standard. Greatness in rushing remains on the Brown standard.

THE MAN IN THE MIDDLE

When I began watching pro football in the 1950s and into the '60s, one of the most important positions on the field was the middle linebacker. Sam Huff, of course, magnified the importance of the position nationally when Walter Cronkite and the CBS TV show *The 20th Century* put a microphone on Huff during a Giants–Bears exhibition game in 1960 as part of a program called "The Violent World of Sam Huff."

It was great TV. It was the first time you heard a ballplayer talk during a game. You heard the collisions, you heard the exchanges between the offense and defense. I remember Huff saying to a Bears player, "What are you doing that for, 88? You do that one more time, 88, I'm going to sock you one. Don't do that again or you'll get a broken nose. Don't hit me on the chin with your elbow."

It was the first time anyone had heard that, unless you were on the field.

The showing of that piece highlighted the position and fans began noticing the middle linebacker. It seems like every team had a great one in the 1960s and '70s. Chuck Bednarik of the Eagles. Ray Nitschke of the Packers. Willie Lanier of the Chiefs. The Falcons had Tommy Nobis, the Baltimore Colts had Mike Curtis and the list goes on. Joe Schmidt of the Lions, Dick Butkus of the Bears, Nick Buoniconti with the Patriots and Dolphins, and of course Huff. These guys were the quarterbacks of the defense.

But today, all of these great players (and most of them are Hall of Famers) wouldn't even play on third down or a passing down. They'd be out of the game, replaced by a defensive back. Two downs and they're out.

Today, the middle linebacker is no big deal. A dinosaur. The game changed.

What's next? Well, without a middle linebacker to block, you see less and less of the fullback. And when you do see them, they're blockers. That's it. You know the path they're headed down.

The middle linebacker, once the most glorified defensive player on the field, has almost become extinct.

84

HELLO, ALLIE

Talked to Allie Sherman, the former Giants coach. He says, "Here's one of the problems in football today. The human factor has been eliminated from the game by technology and computers."

It's all tendencies, what this team does on third down and long or second and short. He says, "What's missing is the coach's touch with the players. Instead, they tell you that you have to do what the computer says. Follow the tendencies."

He feels that's what's wrong with this game and that's an old quarterback talking. When he was coaching the Giants and they were in those championship games in '61, '62, and '63, the rule was that nobody talked in the huddle except the quarterback, which was either the late Charley Conerly or Y.A. Tittle. You could talk on the way back to the huddle but not in it. Allie wouldn't call the plays. He wanted the quarterback to have the feel of the game.

A game plan? Sure. Have one. But he wouldn't interrupt the quarterback's thoughts. Now every play is sent in and the human part of the game is out.

When John Elway played for Dan Reeves, everything was scripted and kept close but when did Elway shine? Late in the game. It's 10–10, they need some points and now they're playing street ball, letting Elway call the plays and stay with the flow of what they were doing.

Which was more exciting? When you think of Elway, what do you think of? Right. Fourth-quarter comebacks engineered by Elway, not game plans printed out from a computer.

Allie coached the Giants from 1961 through '68. Those were colorful times for that team. Allie is one of the great storytellers and that era of the NFL lends itself to his way with words. He was telling me once about the '61 team and the drama that enveloped Y.A. Tittle.

The Giants got Tittle from the 49ers to back up Charley Conerly, who had been with the Giants since 1948 and who, incidentally, should be in the Hall of Fame. Tittle had been with the 49ers for ten years (1951–60) and before that the old Baltimore Colts (1948–50). He had never won a championship game.

So in the '61 season, the Giants tied the Browns 7–7 on the last day of the season to go 10-3-1 and win the Eastern Conference championship. With 20 seconds left in the game, Giants ball, Tittle over center waiting for the snap, the crowd began to count down the clock—16, 15, 14—and as the seconds ticked away, the crowd just got louder and louder. Sherman said everyone could see the tears rolling down the thirty-five-year-old Tittle's face. It was the first time he won a championship game. Keep in mind that only four years earlier Tittle was with the 49ers, who blew a 27–7 third-quarter lead against the Lions in a divisional playoff game and lost 31–27.

When the Giants moved on to play Green Bay on the road for the NFL title, they got one of their ruder shocks in the hotel. Sherman said all of the players and coaches received a very polite phone call in the morning from the hotel operator—"Good morning. Welcome to Titletown, USA. The temperature is eight degrees below zero." Sherman said he was sure Vince Lombardi or someone on his staff had something to do with that little piece of psychological warfare. The Packers won 37–0.

Another NFL great who wasn't above a bit of trickery, Sherman told me, was George Halas. Yes, the Papa Bear himself. In 1963, the Giants played the Bears for the championship and they worked out at Wrigley Field on Friday, two days before the game. They noticed a work crew dressed in white uniforms, cleaning up the stadium, but there was no trash or debris in the stadium because the Bears hadn't played there in almost two weeks. Spies? Well, you never know. But Sherman wasn't taking any chances. He even told the players not to talk football in the hotel elevator because the elevator operators didn't look like the usual union elevator operators.

Then came the biggest surprise. A Chicago paper ran a big headline that said "Giants to Trade Shofner to Green Bay." Well, Sherman had acquired Del Shofner from the Rams in 1961 and had no intention of trading him. He called all the players into his hotel room and said, "Gentlemen, I want to say this in front of the entire team. We are not trading Del Shofner to Green Bay or anyone else. It is a bogus story. It may have come from George Halas and the Bears, to break our concentration. I would not trade Del to Green Bay for Paul Hornung, or even for Paul Hornung and his famous black book."

With that, defensive tackle Dick Modzelewski stands up and says, "Hey, wait a minute, coach. Let's reconsider that."

🎙	**85**

MEN IN STRIPES

Is the NFL officiating getting worse? I don't think so. And I've heard this every year for fifty years.

I say it's the same, or better. You just see more of the controversial plays because of TV and replays. Everything gets replayed from a dozen angles, first on the Jumbotron screens in the stadium, then in your living room. Then the announcers climb aboard the issue, saying the officials missed the call.

People ask, Shouldn't they have full-time officials? That's a funny remark from part-time announcers, who only do play-by-play and color on the weekends, just like the officials. And what good would it do? What are those guys going to do all week, sit around? There are no games during the week, except for the occasional Thursday night game and the Monday night game. Tell me how a referee working full-time in May does his job? There's no games. How is that going to improve things?

You know what I think? The players are too big. You've got these 300-pounders who are also very tall. Maybe the officials can't see around 'em anymore. Add three officials, six more eyes. They haven't added an official since 1978, when they went to seven.

It's like policing the streets. Put enough police officers out there and crime goes down. Get enough eyes watching and maybe there will be fewer penalties and fewer missed calls.

JUST PUCKER UP AND BLOW THE CALL

The worst excuse for a bad call in the NFL is the inadvertent whistle.

Like they're saying, Oops. Sorry. Shouldn't have blown that whistle (or that call). But that's how the NFL weasels out of these controversies—inadvertent whistle. Or the whistle blew the play dead.

Well, the heck with the whistle! The whistle should not be able to cover up a bad call. If the TV replay shows they botched it and the whistle blew before the replay shows that a guy clearly fumbled the ball or before his knee was down, too bad. Stuff the whistle. Remember that play where Jerry Rice fumbled in the playoffs last January against Green Bay on San Francisco's last drive, which led to the winning score? Yeah, the whistle nullified the fumble, the officials let the 49ers keep the ball and they went on to win the game.

I know the NFL brought back instant replay to help the officials, but they can't use it on this kind of play. You want to challenge a call on a play where the side judge gave us a premature whistle? Sorry. You can't do it.

Which actually puts more responsibility on the officials. Instant replay doesn't save them from this particular type of mistake. The whistle cannot be used as an excuse.

I was happy to see the NFL bring back replay for the '99 season on a limited basis. That was the key. Otherwise it got out of hand.

Before, it broke the momentum of the game. Now, except for the last two minutes of each half, when it can be called by the replay official, it's called only by the coaches—two per game. And if the coach is wrong, he pays for it by losing one of his three precious time-outs per half.

However, an inadvertent whistle can still wipe out what otherwise would be a great replay call. So if you blow it, don't blow it.

Another thing that bothers me is when one official throws a flag for defensive pass interference but, after a discussion, another official rules no interference because the ball was not catchable. Well, who says the ball was not catchable? How does he know? Maybe the receiver would have caught the ball if he hadn't been interfered with. I mean, you've never seen a great catch? And if the quarterback sees interference on the play, maybe he throws it differently. Don't try to make the official a mind reader. If it's interference, it's interference, period!

HOLLYWOOD NIGHTS

In 1961 I drove across country in a Fiat. Always wanted to go to California, so I went.

My cousin Mousie (from the Three Stooges) knew this guy who was, get this, Fanny Brice's secretary, and he knew a Hollywood producer. I had always had this idea, this thought, that I could be in the movies as a character actor. I always looked younger than I was—when I was younger. And I wanted to be in the movies. I was always a big movies fan. So they made this arrangement where I could get in to see this producer.

Let me tell you, that meeting was just like in the movies. I went to the offices and it was plush, with a view of the Hollywood Hills. This guy sat behind this huge desk. It might as well have been Louis B. Mayer or David O. Selznick.

So I'm ushered in and he says, "Sit down, young man. What's on your mind?"

So I tell him I think I could be in the movies, play a character part, a young part. I was twenty-three years old and could have passed for eighteen or nineteen. I said I thought I could play some older teenage parts.

He holds up his hands and says, "Just a minute." He pushes a buzzer on his desk, a door opens and this guy comes in. He's about 6-4, maybe twenty-five, twenty-eight years old, and he looked like John Derek, Errol Flynn, Alec Baldwin. Very handsome, Hollywood looks.

The producer says to me, "This is Charlie. He's been in five Broadway shows and he can't get a part in a movie and you're coming in off the street? This isn't the 1930s. You have no chance at all."

And I left.

But I couldn't stop thinking: Does he have this guy Charlie sitting behind that door all day to get rid of guys like me?

I wonder if that guy is still sitting behind the door, now discouraging older guys hoping to get older parts.

And that was the end of my movie career, until 1984, when I was in *Rocky IV*, where I played myself. Love the fights—love the fight movies too.

I remember they are shooting this scene with James Brown, this big musical scene where James sings "Living in America," and it turns out he doesn't know the words. So they get cue cards and Brown is trying to read right off them.

It's a big number, here's how it wraps up: On the last beat of the song, the saxophone player is supposed to come out and throw a cape over James' shoulders. Big finish.

They work on this scene all day, get everything just right, they roll film and at the end the saxophone player comes out and accidentally throws the cape over James' head. Everybody roars.

Stallone comes out and just lies down on the stage floor, like when are we going to get this thing right.

Stallone, who is a perfectionist and has his hand in everything, is a real nice guy and has a lot of patience. I never saw him lose his temper in the ten days of shooting I was there. He has a good sense of humor and the extras who showed up each morning at 5:00 A.M. at $3 a day to fill the MGM Grand seats for the fight scenes loved him.

He would come out and warm them up, telling them how to react during the action shots. A real regular guy, who always had a dream as a kid and fulfilled it.

DON'T I KNOW YOU?

One winter afternoon in New York on the corner of 63rd and Broadway, I saw Robert Duvall standing by himself on the corner. I had always enjoyed his work and followed his career, from when he played at Washington's Arena Stage (before he hit it big in the movies) and lived in Arlington and Alexandria, Virginia. When I saw him this particular day, I had been working in New York about four years.

Before approaching him, I looked all around to make sure no camera was on him. I didn't want to walk into the middle of a shoot. Then I went up to him and said, "Mr. Duvall, I enjoy your work." He said thank you.

Then I said, "I'm Warner Wolf. I used to do the sports on TV at WTOP, Channel 9 in Washington, while you lived in Arlington and Alexandria. Did you ever watch the sports on TV in those days?"

He looked at me and said, "No. I don't remember you in Washington. What do you do in New York?"

Ouch. A double play. He shot me down twice. He didn't remember me from Washington and he doesn't know me from New York.

He's still a great actor and I've never missed any of his pictures—even if he's never heard of me.

MIDDAY COWBOY

Back around 1982, Dustin Hoffman moved into the building I lived in at 10 West 66th Street. He's one of my favorite actors, always has been. I'm coming from the gym, I get in the elevator and there he is. Whoa.

I figure, I'm going to be cool. I'm not going to bother the guy here. That's probably the last thing he wants, to be harassed in his own building. So I punch 32, I lived on the 32nd floor, and he punches 33.

I didn't say a word. I'm thinking. This is good. I'm not bothering him at all, one of the great actors of all time and I'm cool, just letting him be.

But for some reason, as I'm getting out on 32, I put my hands on the door of the elevator and I say, "Do you know who I am?" What a dumb thing to say.

And he says in that Dustin Hoffman mumble, "Ah, no."

I say, "I'm Warner Wolf. I do the sports on Channel 2."

He says, "Well, I'm not here that much." And the doors closed.

Eight years later, Evander Holyfield is fighting Buster Douglas and there's a closed-circuit broadcast at Mickey Mantle's restaurant. And there he is. Dustin Hoffman. I went up to him and just asked if I could take a picture with him. He was the nicest guy. I still have the picture.

I didn't ask him if he knew who I was.

SAFARI, SO GOODY

I took my family to Africa in 1983 to a safari club owned by William Holden. Stephanie Powers has taken it over since. It's in Nairobi, Kenya.

We're eating lunch one day and my daughter Shayna looks at another table and says, "I think that's Robert Redford." And my wife, who never seemed fazed by anybody or ever asked for an autograph, says, "Do you think you could go over there and ask him to pose for a picture?" I said, "What? I can't do that." She says, "I've never asked you in all these years," so I said, "OK." I couldn't turn my wife down.

I was, by the way, wearing this Israeli fatigue hat from a recent trip to Israel. I went over to Redford and he looks up and says, "Warner, who's minding the store?" I couldn't believe it. He knew who I was. He said he had a place on Fifth Avenue and watched Channel 2 when he was in New York. What was he doing in Africa? Scouting production sites for the movie *Out of Africa,* which he was making with Meryl Streep.

So we posed and took pictures, and later I wrote him a letter. I told him my folks were in show business and they always said the bigger the star, the nicer the person. And I told him I was really flattered he knew who I was.

He wrote me back. He said, "Thanks. But it was the fatigue hat that gave you away."

HELLO, JERRY

I saw Jerry Seinfeld at the Reebok Club during the final year of his *Seinfeld* series on NBC and I couldn't resist the opportunity to talk to him.

I went up to him and said, "Jerry, I just want to thank you. My family and I used to see you do standup comedy years ago at Catch a Rising Star and Caroline's. It was great. You were totally clean, always talked about family situations. My girls loved it."

He says thank you.

I paused and said, "So whatever happened to you?" He laughed!

92

SCENE STEALERS

Remember I told you about bumping into Robert Duvall on the street in New York and looking around to see if there were any cameras? Well, I'm not always that careful.

One summer day in 1997, a good friend of mine—Sal Marchiano of WPIX, Channel 11 in New York—and I were having lunch together at a restaurant on Columbus Avenue called Peter's. As we're eating, we see our old friends Danny Aiello and another actor, Paulie Herman, walking along Columbus Avenue.

Sal and I get up from the table, go outside, and start talking to Danny and Paulie. We notice that they are not exactly greeting us with open arms. We ask, "What's wrong?" They point across the street.

There, on the other side of Columbus Avenue, is a huge camera and a crew. They were shooting an episode of *Dellaventura* for CBS.

Sal and I spoiled their shot.

Another time, I was walking by 72nd Street between Amsterdam and Broadway. Meg Ryan and Tom Hanks were filming *You've Got Mail.* As I'm watching, I see a guy completely dressed in a tennis outfit, with a racquet in his hand.

Since I play tennis, I said, "Hey, where do you play?" He said, "I don't play. I'm in the movie. I'm waiting for my scene."

Point, set and match.

Then in August of 1999, one week after I had seen the remake of *The Thomas Crown Affair,* I took my five-year-old granddaughter, Samantha, to the Central Park Zoo. As we were getting animal food from one of the quarter machines, I look up, and who's standing next to me but Pierce Brosnan—of *Thomas Crown* and, of course, the James Bond series. I shook his hand, said, "I enjoy your work." He said, "Thank you." He looked like the average guy at the zoo with his kids.

By the way—just for the record—he was not filming a scene, and I did not ask him if he knew who I was. It took a long time, but I've finally learned.

He was very cordial. And I must say: It's the only time where I liked a remake more than the original.

TAKE MY COMEDIAN, PLEASE

Robert Merrill, the great Metropolitan Opera star, is in Miami and he bumps into Henny Youngman. Henny says, "What are you doing here?" Merrill says, "I'm performing *The Barber of Seville*." Henny says, "I've never seen an opera. Would you leave me tickets?" Merrill says, "Sure."

After the first act, there's a knock at his dressing room door. It's Henny Youngman.

He opens the door, says, "Henny, how'd you like it?"

Henny says, "I couldn't understand a word."

That was Henny Youngman. Henny went to a ballet once. He's watching the ballerinas dancing on their toes. He turns to the guy next to him and says, "Why don't they just get taller girls?"

One time my daughter Shayna and I were eating at the Carnegie Deli on Seventh Ave. Henny is at another table. He looks at my daughter reading the menu and says, "There's no plot."

At Henny's funeral, they told this story: His rabbi came to visit him at the hospital and Henny motions for his rabbi to bend down so he can whisper to him. Henny says, "Rabbi, these doctors are all crooks."

The rabbi says, "Henny, why do you think that?"

"Because they all wear masks."

Why mention Henny Youngman? Well, unbeknownst to him, Henny Youngman had an unusual influence on my life. I had read in the paper that Henny—who had never been bar mitzvahed—decided to do so at the age of eighty in Atlantic City. Since I had never been bar mitzvahed either, I figured that if it wasn't too late for him, it wasn't too late for me. So after studying one year with Cantor Seymour Schwarzmer of Mount Vernon, New York, I was bar mitzvahed on June 21, 1986, in Greenwich, Connecticut. I was forty-eight.

And just for the record: In December of 1999, as this book was going to press, Kirk Douglas was bar mitzvahed on his birthday. He was eighty-three.

MY PICKS AT THE FLICKS

You want to get a good argument going in a bar? Bring up sports movies. Everybody's got a favorite.

Baseball has probably spawned more films than any other sport. Its grasp on the American public dates to the time Hollywood became a big industry, when pro football wasn't big and there wasn't any NBA. The sports heroes came from college football, boxing and especially baseball.

People of a certain generation won't back off in any discussion of sports movies. They're going with *Pride of the Yankees,* the story of Lou Gehrig's life. Big tearjerker, tragic ending. But one funny thing about it—Gary Cooper batted right-handed and had to be shot with a mirror when he was hitting so he'd look like Gehrig. The New York or Yankees inscription on his shirt had to be sewn on backwards.

The 1948 *Babe Ruth Story,* with William Bendix, a fine character actor, would not make it today—it's too corny for today's audiences, and the film obviously left out Ruth's dark side.

More of these old baseball films made sure the players were heroic. Often they involved triumph over tragedy. Like *The Stratton Story*, about Monty Stratton (starring Jimmy Stewart). Stratton, a White Sox pitcher, accidentally shot off a toe in a hunting accident and was never the same though he did return to pitch in the majors. Ronald Reagan played Grover Cleveland Alexander and Frank Lovejoy played Rogers Hornsby in *The Winning Team*. I liked Robert Redford in *The Natural*. He looked "natural" as a pitcher and as a hitter. And who could forget Anthony Perkins as Jimmy Piersall and Karl Malden as the overbearing father in *Fear Strikes Out*? Certainly *Field of Dreams* was great, but that was more a human interest, nostalgic story than a sustained depiction of realistic baseball action.

If I had to pick four of the best-made baseball movies, the ones where it at least looked like baseball players were involved in making the film. I'd go with *Pride of the Yankees, The Natural, Eight Men Out,* which was the story of the 1919 Black Sox scandal, and one which is not well known, called *Tiger Town*. That was made by Disney and starred Roy Scheider. Better known for his roles in *The French Connection, Marathon Man, Jaws* and *All That Jazz,* Scheider played an aging outfielder with the Detroit Tigers.

After watching this film, I was extremely impressed with how natural Scheider looked with the bat. Unlike Gary Cooper or William Bendix, Scheider actually looked like a ballplayer. He was believable. So I figured he must have played a lot of ball before he became an actor.

And that's what I thought until I ran into him at an HBO dinner. When I asked him about it, he said no. He had been a boxer but he wasn't a ballplayer. But to get into character and look like one, he spent one entire summer working at Tiger Stadium, when the Tigers were on the road.

Gates Brown, who had been one of the great pinch hitters in American League history, taught him how to hit. Scheider worked out with Brown for three or four hours a day. Toward the end of the summer, Scheider said he really began to hit the ball and was looking pretty good at bat. Well, it just so happened that one day, with Brown not around, Scheider was using the automatic pitching machine, which we used to call "Overhand Joe." After hitting a few balls around the infield, Scheider said he really got hold of one, meeting the ball on the fat, or sweet, part of the bat. The ball took off, his best shot of the summer.

A long drive to deep left field—back, back, back, BOOM!—the ball actually hit the 340 sign in deep left, just missing a home run by a few feet. Scheider said he was elated. But as he started to celebrate, he looked around the park and realized no one was there except 52,415 empty seats. No ushers, no vendors, no grounds crew, no Gates Brown, no cameras, no nothing. The longest ball he had ever hit in his life and nobody saw it.

I usually enjoy films about boxing, which, as you know by now, was the first sport I really followed. I remember Errol Flynn as James J. Corbett in *Gentleman Jim,* which also starred Ward Bond as John L. Sullivan. There was John Garfield in *Body and Soul.* James Cagney in *City for Conquest. The Harder They Fall,* with Humphrey Bogart and Rod Steiger (and also Max Baer Sr. and Jersey Joe Walcott).

The one that sticks in most people's minds is *Requiem for a Heavyweight,* which starred Anthony Quinn as Mountain Rivera. This was a loose portrayal of the career of heavyweight champion Primo Carnera, who was controlled by the mob and was, unfortunately, not a good fighter. He was champion for only one year. You know who had a part in that movie, as the young and upcoming challenger? Muhammad Ali. Of course he was Cassius Clay then, two years before he beat Sonny Liston for the title.

Kirk Douglas was very believable as middleweight Midge Kelly in *Champion*. Robert Ryan showed the seamy side of boxing as Stoker Thompson in *The Set-Up*.

The five *Rocky* movies, which were probably three too many, played off the success of the first. The original was so enjoyable that you overlooked the fact that no referee in the world would have let the fight continue. No fighter could take that much punishment and not collapse. And that's the way it went through four more films, with Rocky Balboa (Sylvester Stallone) getting beat up but ultimately triumphing over Apollo Creed (Carl Weathers), Clubber Lang (Mr. T) and the Russian champion played by Dolph Lundgren.

Without question the film that sets the standard for all boxing films from now on is *Raging Bull*, with Robert De Niro as middleweight champion Jake LaMotta. It doesn't get any better. The movie pulled no punches, not in the ring scenes or in its look at LaMotta's hard life.

My thumbnail rundowns of films by sports:

Basketball: Some good ones, such as *Hoop Dreams* and *He Got Game*. I enjoyed both, plus *Hoosiers,* with Gene Hackman.

Hockey: *Slap Shot,* with Paul Newman, is about it, unless you're into the Mighty Ducks.

Golf: *The Ben Hogan Story* starred Glenn Ford. *Tin Cup* wasn't bad.

Track: *Chariots of Fire* won lots of awards, including best picture, and focused on friendship as much as sports.

You'd think there would be more and better movies about football. And you'd be wrong. Sure, there's Burt Lancaster as Jim Thorpe, Tony Curtis in *The All American,* Doc Blanchard and Glenn Davis as themselves in a tribute to Army football, Pat O'Brien as Knute Rockne (and Ronald Reagan as George Gipp).

Black Sunday, with Robert Shaw. *Pigskin Parade* with Judy Garland and Jack Haley. You'll still get a laugh from the Marx Brothers' take on college football in *Horse Feathers.* There was Mac Davis loosely portraying a version of Don Meredith in *North Dallas Forty,* or *Jerry McGuire* with Tom Cruise and Cuba Gooding Jr.

Probably the two best football films were *The Longest Yard* with Burt Reynolds and *Rudy.*

A few others I liked: *The Hustler,* which is about as good a movie as you'll see and is about a lot of things as much as it is about shooting pool; and *Phar Lap,* about a top racehorse.

Did I miss one you really enjoyed—*Bang the Drum Slowly, Bingo Long, It Happens Every Spring, Angels in the Outfield, Fast Break, The Fish That Saved Pittsburgh?* That's the great thing about movie trivia. Everybody has their likes and dislikes and nobody can tell you you're wrong.

CHOPPER ALERT

Everybody in the television business can tell a story where something went wrong and left them open for ridicule or humiliation. I've had my share, but the most embarrassing was in the summer of 1998.

I had these two front teeth that were on posts, that I always had trouble with. Went to the dentist, he said he could make a bridge. I wore the temporary bridge for three months, went back to the dentist, he says, "Good news, I've got the regular ones. But I'm not going to put them in permanently. I'm going to put them in with a temporary glue so you can see how they feel for a couple of weeks."

I'm on the air three nights later, a Friday night. Just wrapping up, I always close with a horse race, I say, "Let's go to the videotape" and BOOM! The bridge falls out. Six teeth gone.

Fortunately, the race comes up, I shove the bridge back in,

but not quick enough. It was all over the newspapers and TV. I even made *Entertainment Tonight.*

So when I came back on the air Monday, I brought a pair of those chattering teeth, wound them up, and when the anchorwoman, Dana Adams, introduced me, I put 'em on the table and said, "How come these things have been following me around?" Everyone in the studio roared.

It all goes back to what my father told me as a youngster: "If you can't laugh at yourself, you don't have a right to laugh at anyone else."

ALL SPORTS, ALL THE TIME

Without question, ESPN changed the face of sportscasting. Imagine that, sports around the clock. The news when you want it, as it happens. I know it had a dramatic impact on my business, really made local stations rethink what they were doing.

It didn't so much affect the 6:00 P.M. shows but it really made a difference at eleven o'clock when you gave your audience the sports news of the night.

When I began doing the eleven o'clock sports in Washington and New York in the '60s and '70s, where you were giving the late-night scores, there was always a good chance it was the first time the viewers got the results. Today? Guess again. By the time you get on the air at 11:20 P.M., there is no way the real sports fan does not know the score of the games. Thank you very much, ESPN.

Oh, your highlights may be different and better for that particular local market team than ESPN's, because you can

259

stay longer on the local highlights. ESPN can't, because its aim is national and it broadcasts to the entire country. So ESPN has to show fewer of each team's highlights to cover the bigger picture.

I certainly don't want to take any credit for anything ESPN does and does well, but I believe I'm the guy who first put the emphasis on all these highlights, including out-of-town stuff. Yep, over thirty years ago I began doing it in Washington. In 1968. By 1978, everyone was doing it.

Hey, once it's on TV, it practically becomes public domain. Your approach gets copied. You can be cloned.

In 1983, I was put on the *CBS Morning News* with Bill Kurtis and Diane Sawyer on Friday mornings. My boss at the time, Neil Derrough, who was the general manager at WCBS in New York, asked me one day, "Warner, do you realize what has happened because of your appearances on the *CBS Morning News,* which goes out all over the country? You've blown the cover of all the other sportscasters in the other markets, who were stealing your stuff."

I wondered. Would people think their local guy stole from me or that I stole from him? Keep in mind it's a compliment when someone borrows your act, but I wondered if people would get tired of seeing so many highlights. But I don't think they do. A sports fan can watch the same play over and over.

Look at Franco Harris' 1972 touchdown vs. the Raiders, known as the Immaculate Reception. It's been shown 10,000 times, but whenever it's on I stop and look at it. Or Doug Flutie's Hail Mary pass against the University of Miami, Thanksgiving of 1984. Or the film of Bobby Thomson's home run. Or Jerry West's desperation shot against the

Knicks in the third game of the 1970 NBA championship, which sent the game to overtime.

We watch. Over and over. Do we think Harris won't score or Flutie will get sacked or that West's shot won't go in? That's the way people are. They never get tired of great plays. They never get tired of highlights.

That's good enough for me. You know where I'm going with this—to the videotape!

JOCKS IN THE BOOTH

They're everywhere, the former athletes toting a mike on TV. The experience that counts for them is on the field, not in this second profession.

Let me point out one thing here. There is a huge difference between being a play-by-play man and an analyst, and another between those jobs and handling the sportscast on the six and eleven o'clock news.

How many players who went into doing play-by-play have lasted? Tim McCarver, Ralph Kiner, Ken Harrelson, Bobby Murcer, Jim Katt, Ken Singleton, Mike Shannon, Bob Uecker, to name a few. All of them were *baseball* players doing baseball play-by-play. There aren't many former basketball players or football players or hockey players who do play-by-play in their sport. Pat Summerall, Hot Rod Hundley and Tom Heinsohn are a few of the exceptions.

And how many ex-players are doing the six and eleven o'clock news? A low percentage. Why? Because while they were growing up, devoting most of their time and energy to playing their particular sport, other guys—nonathletes, like me—were growing up following all sports. This, I think, is why they tend to survive as analysts for the sport they played.

I have done play-by-play in baseball, football and basketball and always felt fortunate to have an ex-player working alongside of me. He made my job more interesting by giving insight an announcer could not give, because he played the game. The key was to bring the player into the broadcast and ask him how he reacted in that particular situation, what he saw or how the play should have been made. It's something his nonathlete fellow announcer couldn't do.

I worked with a lot of former players who served as analysts—Bob Gibson was terrific. He could take a game apart from the pitcher's point of view, what he was trying to do, what the batter might be looking for, what he thought of the manager or catcher coming out to the mound. I enjoyed working with Gibson and getting the benefit of his years of experience and insights.

The biggest difference between now and thirty years ago is that you have to be good. It's not enough to just be who you are, or who you were. The fans are too knowledgeable today and there are too many guys who can provide excellent and entertaining analysis. The ex-athlete can't just hang his hat on what he did on the field. Now he's competing with other ex-athletes who are good on the air.

Back when I was getting started, the executives picked a big-name ex-player and that was it. Whether he was any good on the air was secondary. Now there's pressure to be good or be gone.

As you know, every football player faces the day when

some team representative tells him he's wanted in the coach's office and to bring his playbook. They know that's the end. Maybe we'll see the day when there's a knock on the door and a voice says to the ex-athlete in the TV booth, "The station general manager wants to see you. . . . And bring your microphone."

98

PLAY-BY-PLAY

ABC was showing baseball on a national basis and they put me on with Bob Prince, the longtime voice of the Pittsburgh Pirates, and Bob Uecker. We would split the play-by-play. Then ABC said they couldn't tell me from Uecker, which one of us was talking. So they split us up. That's when Al Michaels came in.

The big thrill for me was doing the 1976 All-Star Game. It was the first one I covered, though I had gone to the '56 All-Star Game at Griffith Stadium with my father. Mantle, Williams, Mays and Musial all homered in that game. In '76 you had all the Reds—Joe Morgan, Johnny Bench, Pete Rose—and the sense of really being surrounded by greatness.

People ask about the difference between doing play-by-play on radio and on television. There's no question about it, you really have to be good to do radio play-by-play. You don't have to be that good on television, where the picture speaks for itself. On radio, you are the eyes of the listener. You have to be on top of it and follow everything. I think all the good ones today on TV came from radio.

Some people think basketball is the hardest game to do play-by-play for because the pace is so fast, but I think it's the easiest. There's only ten men on the court at one time and there's only twelve on each team. If you do the same team each week, there's a lot fewer numbers to memorize and maybe only eight guys from each team will get in the game. In football, you've got over a hundred to memorize, fifty-three from each side. In baseball? Fifty. I always thought basketball was easiest because the only pauses occurred at time-outs and then you didn't have to talk because you went to a commercial.

I thought baseball and football were much more difficult because you had so many pauses, either between pitches or during huddles.

I never did play-by-play for hockey, only color, but again, fewer players in action at one time and no pauses. Only five skaters and one goalie, and it could be less if a team was shorthanded. For me, basketball was the easiest. Fewer players and numbers.

And speaking of play-by-play, on January 24, 1991, I flew to Israel during the Gulf War. A friend of mine, Menashe Raz, asked if I would come over, bring my plays of the year and appear on Israeli TV—as a sort of comic relief to help entertain people during the war. To my surprise, Menashe also said that Israeli TV would be bringing in the Giants–Bills Super Bowl. It was just the picture—no sound—and Menashe asked me if I would do the color in English while Uri Levy did the play-by-play in Hebrew.

A first: two men in the booth, two languages!

Now, considering Israel is only the size of New Jersey, at that time—except for CNN—there was no station on other than Israeli TV. So after the game Menashe said to me, "Warner, you had a captive audience! You were on coast to coast."

THE ART OF INTERVIEWING

The biggest single ingredient in a successful interview is preparation. BE PREPARED! Do your homework before the interview begins. It makes you look good and, just as important, makes the interviewee feel that you know your stuff and have taken the time to find out about him. It's a type of flattery for the subject of your interview.

Also, try to keep the questions relatively short and phrased so that the person being interviewed must give the responses and can't just say "right" or "yes" or "no" to your questions. It makes you appreciate the talkers. When Joe Theismann was playing for the Redskins, you only had to ask one question and he would pretty much conduct the rest of the interview.

I have always tried to treat my subject as a guest. I invited him. I always try to treat him fairly and with respect. You don't have to like the guy or his performance on the field or what he stands for but you should put that aside during the interview.

Also, don't say "I think this" or "I think that, do you agree?" Don't put the person on the spot to disagree with you. That's not what we're here for. Say, "What do you think?" That way you get the person's thoughts whether or not he agrees with you. This is one of the things that made Johnny Carson so great. He gave the guest the spotlight. He also didn't interrupt the guest. He let them finish and he listened.

A lot of interviewers cut off their guest so they can get in their next question. NO GOOD! Let the guest finish. And don't fink out by saying, "A lot of people say" or "A lot of people think" or "A lot of people accuse you of . . ." Just ask the question. Are you? Did you? Tell us about it.

At the end, there's nothing wrong with saying "Thank you" or "Thank you for coming." It's like telling your guest goodbye. It's a nice finish and it's polite. You should always be polite to your guests, no matter how you feel about them.

INSTANT ACCESS

When I first got started in the business, you could pick up the phone and call any hotel a team was staying in and get ahold of whomever you wanted. Really. There were no bodyguards or entourages or guys registering under phony names.

Nineteen sixty-five, ball game between the Dodgers and Giants, Juan Marichal hits John Roseboro, the Dodgers catcher, over the head with a bat. Next day I called the operator at the Roosevelt Hotel in New York, where the Dodgers were staying before a series with the Mets. I asked her to put us through to Sandy Koufax' room and she did. And he picked up the phone.

He pitched in that game so we told him we were recording the call and could he describe the incident for us and he did.

Today? You'd have no chance. They'd be screening the calls.

I used to take my small tape recorder to the team hotels and interview the visiting ballplayers. They were just sitting around the lobby. All the American League visiting teams in Washington—except the White Sox—stayed at the Shoreham Hotel. Today they don't sit around the lobby, they have other things to do. It was great then, like a smorgasbord. You'd get to the hotel around 11:00 A.M. and there they were, all the players sitting in the lobby. Over the years I must have recorded over 100 interviews for my old radio show. Tape it Saturday morning, then play it Monday through Friday.

One time, former AL outfielder Wally Moses, a good hitter and later a hitting instructor, takes me aside at the Shoreham, stands me in front of a mirror in the hotel lobby and says, "Let me see your stance and stroke." I show him. And he politely says, "Not bad. But you need help."

Of course today's players probably need to be protected more from these autograph hunters than the press. Guys would always sign your ball. They didn't care. Nobody was going to take that ball and sell it. You would keep it for yourself. I had Roger Maris on my show and I got his autograph, and Mickey Mantle and Hank Aaron and none of them ever looked at me funny or wondered what I was going to do with the ball. Because there wasn't any question. It was for me. Today, you sign a ball and the guy's going to sell it at a card show.

But don't get mad at the players for signing things at card shows. If this is the way things are, then they should get paid. I have no problem with that. When you put an autograph on a ball, it means something. If the player signs a ball for you, it means something beyond whatever monetary value it might have. If Yogi Berra signs your ball, you got that autograph from a player you admire. If you sell it to someone, all that person gets is a ball with writing on it. It's a big business today.

In 1974, when I was at WTOP in Washington, we wanted to do a story on the designated hitter. The rule had been put into effect the year before and, in case you're wondering, the Yankees' Ron Blomberg was the first DH ever to come to bat. Well, we were without a team in Washington, again. Remember, the Senators, the second Senators team, had gone off to become the Texas Rangers in 1972. To do the story, we had to go to Baltimore. The angle we wanted was what the DH does during the game, between at bats and during the innings, since he isn't on the field.

I called the Orioles and left a message for Tommy Davis, who had been a two-time batting champion with the Dodgers (1962 and 1963). Davis, who was now thirty-five, was the Orioles DH. He calls me back and says he'll do it, he'll let us follow him around, but he wants $100. I asked my news director, Jim Snyder, and he says, "Sure, it's worth it. Give him the $100."

So the cameraman and I drive over to Baltimore. We shoot Davis on the bench. We even shoot Davis in the clubhouse, and he talks about reading magazines between innings, watching TV, swinging bats. It's great. Complete access. All for $100.

We didn't have to get permission from major league baseball or the commissioner's office. We just went in and shot the story (and delivered the dough, of course).

Maybe Tommy Davis was the first athlete to utter those immortal words—Show me the money.

WASHINGTON AND NEW YORK—
MORE THAN MILES APART

As I said before, the biggest difference in these cities as markets is that in New York there's always something going on. And the reason is, you have two basketball teams, two football teams, two baseball teams, three hockey teams. And that's just the professionals. Then you have the colleges, St. John's and the others. And then you have everybody and anybody who wants to publicize something coming through, whether it's a fight or someone who has written a book, players named to a Hall of Fame, there's always something.

One spring afternoon, the Miami Heat were in town to play the New Jersey Nets and the Nets had just made two big trades, one with Dallas. So in the morning I went and interviewed Pat Riley because the Heat were working out at the Reebok Club in New York. Then I went to the Meadowlands and interviewed John Calipari of the Nets about the trades. And later in the day the New York Jets had an event to promote a charity. And later still there was a card signing thing and Catfish Hunter was there. Wow, four stories in one day.

One afternoon last February, during what could have been a slow sports day, I interviewed Charles Oakley, back in New York for his first game against the Knicks. Then had George Steinbrenner, talking about losing a salary arbitration hearing with Derek Jeter that gave Jeter the second highest salary ever awarded, $5 million. And then Tim McCarver, who had just joined the Yankees' broadcast team after the Mets replaced him with Tom Seaver. I don't know about eight million stories in the naked city—but there are always plenty of sports stories.

THE WORST RATING EVER

I'd been on the air about a week during my first stay in New York in 1976, and I received a box. Didn't know who it was from or what was in it. So I opened it up.

It was a piece of toilet paper, used. Had a brown spot on it. With a note that said, "This is what we think of you. Members of the senior class, Union City New Jersey High."

Man, I could do no wrong in Washington, but New York? What a rough town. I guess it really was going from the penthouse to the outhouse.

BILL COMES DUE

In October of 1998 I interviewed Bill Bradley about his book *Values of the Game*. We talked about the old Knicks and the late Red Holzman and how the game has changed. One big difference—Holzman actually would call a time-out to let the players call the play.

It sounds unbelievable but you have to remember Red had Dave DeBusschere, who had been a player-coach, and Bradley, who was a Rhodes Scholar, and Willis Reed, who later coached the Knicks.

As the interview wound down, I asked Bradley, a former senator from New Jersey, if he was going to begin the run for President in November 1999. He said he would decide in three weeks but I would be the first to know.

On the night he decided to form an exploratory committee, a key step in the process of seeking the nomination, I came on the air and played the tape and said, "Come on. He never called. Boo!"

That may be the first time Bill Bradley ever got booed in New York.

 **104**

GOOD TASTE

Had a news director in Washington named Jim Snyder. He told me one time, when I asked him about using something risqué, that I should follow a simple rule. If you have to ask, don't do it. Good rule.

The news director at WABC in New York in the late '70s was Ron Tindiglia. He was a cheerleader. He would jump up and down when you walked past his office. Loved charts. Had charts with all the ratings. His Channel 4 chart said, "News for the dead." His chart for Channel 2 said, "The cheap imitators." For us at Channel 7? "The kings." And that's the way it was, because the ratings were so good.

Ron would watch every show and recall everything you said on the air. He and Snyder were both very good communicators with the talent on the show. And neither one had any jealousy about not being on the air themselves. That's sometimes a problem with news directors. They can be wannabes or have-to-bes. Not these guys. They were the best I ever had.

We didn't have outside consultants. There was no such thing. Jim and Ron were so confident in their judgment that the idea of bringing in an outsider was the last thing on their minds. How could a guy from Iowa tell a guy from New York or Washington what was right? That's one of the big changes now: There were no outside consultants, because we figured, Who knew the station better than the news director?

We had it going good at WABC. Ron brought in Spencer Christian, who had worked in Baltimore and Richmond, to do the weather and Larry Kane from Philadelphia to anchor the show, and the chemistry was great.

Larry was rapid-fire, kept a great pace, and the eleven o'clock show really took off. I used to joke around with Spencer Christian. He'd go to the map and point out all these cities: "It's 45 in Hackensack, 43 in Bayonne" and I'd yell out, "What about us?" And he'd keep pointing and say, "They're asking what about us in Peekskill. It's 46 in Peekskill." I'd walk down the street, people would see me and yell out, "What about us?"

We were together from 1977 to about 1980 but Larry got homesick for Philadelphia. He never lived in New York. He commuted from Philadelphia, had a driver waiting for him outside the studio, after every show.

I always felt he could have been a huge anchorman in New York but he wanted to go back to Philadelphia and that's what he did, working now for KYW-TV. You know what I should have said to him when he left? "What about us?"

A HELPING HAND

One thing that's very important in this business is to have a good producer. I have been very fortunate, working with the late Carmine Cincotta for sixteen years, Cliff Gelb for fifteen years and Larry Duvall, Rich Trueman and Nick Juliano for three years. These are guys you can rely on on a daily basis. Make sure everything is right, *before* you go on the air.

Let me tell you a story about Cliff Gelb.

It's January 1990 and the 49ers have just crushed the Broncos 55–10 in the Super Bowl. The station asked me to come in to do the late sports show that Sunday evening, because CBS had broadcast the game. I said sure. And to analyze the game I brought in former Giants coach Allie Sherman.

Allie was great. We showed highlights and he gave his insights, pointing out what the 49ers were doing right (everything) and what the Broncos were messing up (everything).

The best part was that we had almost no time limit, since we didn't go on until after midnight. The 11:00 P.M. producer told us to go as long as we wanted because the show was open-ended, meaning that although we couldn't talk all night, there was no network show that followed us at a designated time.

So Allie and I did about seven minutes on the Super Bowl (and that's pretty long for TV) and threw it back to the anchor people.

I had no idea at this point that Cliff had shown the kind of cool under pressure that you would expect from Joe Montana. After the show, Cliff told me that about halfway through the Sherman interview, the news director, who didn't know a football from a donut, called the control room to say the interview was running too long and to "get 'em off." Cliff, in what I consider a stroke of genius, told him that the interview with Sherman was on tape and we couldn't cut out early.

The news director reluctantly said OK, accepted Cliff's explanation and hung up.

Thanks to Cliff, those fans who tuned in specifically for a critique of the Super Bowl were saved from being short-changed. And that's why guys like me owe a lot to guys like Cliff.

Once again, you must always remember that it's YOUR face the people see on the screen—not the news director's, not the producer's. If the show looks bad, YOU look bad. On the other hand, if the show looks good, YOU look good.

RATINGS, RANTINGS AND RAVINGS

I have always felt the three month-long rating periods for local news stations all over the country—February, May and November—are overrated. These are the three months out of the year where the ratings are taken for the station and serve as the base for the rates that the stations can charge the advertisers.

During these three months, stations around the country will run what they call sweeps specials. Investigative reports that could run for a week at a time. My question is this: What about the other nine months of the year? Do you think a viewer is going to suddenly turn on your station because of a sweeps special if he's not already watching you the other nine months of the year? If stations put as much effort into the other nine months as into the three ratings months, they'd do much better.

It seems to me that if you get people to watch you the other nine months, they will continue to watch you the other three months, whether you have a sweeps special or not. It's as if the emphasis is in the wrong place.

Another thing I have never agreed with: Some people in charge will tell you it's not good to repeat a sports piece on the 11:00 P.M. show if you ran it at 6:00 P.M. My argument: Except for people in the business, whose job it is to watch every show, the average person is not going to see both. It's a different audience.

First of all, in cities like New York or Washington, not everybody is at home at six o'clock to watch the news. They're still in their cars or riding the train, commuting from their jobs, picking up their kids. And for the people that do get home by six, there's a pretty good chance they are not going to wait up for your 11:00 P.M. news. They're already asleep or they've already watched the ten o'clock news.

With cable and *Seinfeld* reruns at 11:00 P.M., the days of getting the same audience at six and eleven are long gone. Again, except for those in the business who are paid to watch both shows, I bet you're broadcasting to an 85 percent different audience at six and eleven. Therefore, if you have a great sports piece, interview or highlight at six, why cheat one audience by not playing it again at eleven? The fact is, although the news usually doesn't change much from seven to eleven and the weather forecast probably stays the same, most of the sports report will be different simply because the games are played between seven and eleven o'clock.

🎙 107

OPEN MOUTH, INSERT FOOT

When I first joined WABC-TV (Channel 7) in New York to do the 6:00 P.M. local news, as well as my network assignments, the general manager of the station, Ken McQueen, brought me in to the ABC corporate offices. This was going to be a big meet-and-greet, over on 54th and Sixth Avenue, with the president of the owned-and-operated stations, a fellow named Dick O'Leary.

O'Leary had been there for years and was instrumental in helping get WABC to the top, so of course I'm there to make a good impression and assure him I'm going to be a big plus for the station and the network.

After talking for about five minutes, O'Leary asked me if there was anything on my mind.

This probably would have been a good time for me to say no. I said yes.

"You know those little round gold circles we have to wear on the air, with a 7 inside the circle?" I began. "I think that's corny. It takes away from the individuality of the performer. Like it's kindergarten, if we got lost our parents would know where to find us. It also sticks holes in our jackets. And why do we all have to wear the same dark blue blazers on the air? Why can't we wear our own clothes instead of the same old Channel 7 ABC blazers?"

Well, that was the last question I got to ask for the next ten minutes.

O'Leary jumps out of his seat and starts screaming at me.

"I'm the reason you wear the circle 7 pins," he yelled. "And it was also my idea for all the on-the-air people to wear the blazers. The circle 7 pin is worn by everyone in the United States who works at an owned-and-operated ABC station. It reminds the people at home they are watching Channel 7."

He wasn't done yet.

"And as far as the blazers go, I did that because guys like you wouldn't know how to dress!"

You should have seen him. His face was as red as a stop sign. It was like I had attacked his family, which I guess in a way he thought I had.

As a parting shot he said, "And what do you know, coming from Washington, telling a guy like me what to do?"

I glanced over at McQueen, who was a real nice guy, and McQueen said, "Well, Dick, I think we'd better go. Warner has to prepare for the six o'clock news."

We left O'Leary's office and walked down the hall. Mc-Queen turned to me and said, "Warner, in all my years in the business, this was the first time I thought I was going to see someone hired and fired the same day."

OUR WAY OR THE HIGHWAY

Whenever I think of the college football scoreboard, I relive my two brief years on the ABC network show. I guess ABC Sports just didn't appreciate my perspective on how the show should be done.

Instead of just giving the winners and losers and the scores—keep in mind in 1975 and '76 we didn't have as many highlights of games, if any at all—I would say things like, "Notre Dame, a 14-point favorite, won the game but lost the point spread, beating Michigan State by only seven points."

Or, "The Boo of the Week goes to Woody Hayes, for kicking a field goal in the fourth quarter with a 35–0 lead."

I thought it livened up the show and made it different. The network didn't!

It was good for local TV but not for the network. I disagreed and was off the show after two years. So if you had Warner Wolf and the *ABC College Football Scoreboard* and three years—YOU LOST!

MARATHON MEN, WOMEN
AND CHILDREN

I certainly admire anyone who devotes the time and effort to prepare for a marathon. I mean, training to run twenty-six miles? It's even more unbelievable for the disabled and the wheelchair participants, who should get a medal just for finishing.

Obviously it's not a sport we cover a lot, but we certainly do pay attention to the New York City Marathon each fall. All those people coming out to run, or cheer the runners, or give them water and oranges just makes for a special day in the city.

My best marathon memory takes me back to 1977, when WABC, Channel 7, had the foresight to keep its camera crew at the finish line well past midnight, more than twelve hours after the start. That enabled us to film a young woman on crutches walking over the finish line in the dark and cold. It was a terrific human interest story as well as a good TV story, which we used the next day on the six and eleven o'clock news (there was no noon or five o'clock broadcast in those days).

Most people tend to remember the Rosie Ruiz marathon, where the women's winner was found to have taken a short-cut and was disqualified.

I had a great view of the marathon from my apartment on 66th and Central Park West. I could look out right at the finish line. It was kind of funny actually, to step out on the balcony and see the runners crossing the finish line, and then being able to go back inside and see it on TV.

But as far as caring who won? It didn't make any difference to me. I didn't know any of the runners except for our weatherman at Channel 2, Mr. G.—Irv Gikofsky—and we all knew there was no way he was going to win.

Gotta give him credit, though. Mr. G., who's in his fifties, still runs the marathon. He should be crossing the finish line just about . . . now.

FRANK FIELD SAVED FROM CHOKING

People love to bash television as a vast wasteland, but I have to disagree. You can learn a lot about all sorts of things and you never know when that knowledge you absorbed just by paying a little attention can make a big difference.

In 1985, Frank Field and I went out to dinner at a place on Eleventh Avenue called the Landmark Tavern. Frank was a very popular weatherman in New York, nice guy, about ten years older than I am.

Frank's having roast beef and I look across the table and I say, "Man, you really eat big pieces. You don't cut your meat into small pieces." He says, "Ah, that's the way I've always eaten."

Next time I look up he's gagging and he has this ashen gray face, the worst color I've ever seen on a living person. He's pointing to his throat.

One second he's fine, ten seconds later, this. I got up, walked around him in this very crowded restaurant, he stood up, I got behind him and put my arms around his abdomen and started pulling with these very hard thrusts. On the third one, the piece of roast beef flew out. We both sat down.

The whole thing was over in like ten seconds. No one in the whole place had moved. Frank was sitting there, mopping perspiration from his face.

Now the only reason I knew about the Heimlich maneuver was because five years before, when he worked at NBC as the medical reporter as well as the weatherman, he had done a whole series on the Heimlich maneuver. And I had watched his series on TV. And because I had learned the Heimlich maneuver from him, I was able to use it on him.

Finally, Frank says, "What took you so long?" I said, "What do you mean?" He looks me right in the eye and says, "My entire life, my family, flashed across my mind while you were doing that. You must have taken three minutes to get over here and do that."

I said, "Frank, it was over in ten seconds. If it took me three minutes you'd be dead."

WORLD SERIES ROUNDUP

I hate to say it, but there seemed to be a double standard for many of the New York media—of which I am a member—in their treatment of Mets manager Bobby Valentine and Yankee skipper Joe Torre. During the regular season, following a Yankee loss in which Derek Jeter—in a mild slump at the plate—committed an error on the field, Torre was asked by a TV producer whether his shortstop was maybe losing his concentration. Torre, a terrific guy on and off the field, especially with the press following a game, uncharacteristically lashed out: "You should be ashamed of yourself for asking that question, and you should know better!" Well, nobody chastised Torre for his comment. Instead, the take was that he was sticking up for his players—which is okay.

But one month later, after the Mets had lost 7 in a row—and 8 of 9 in a 10-day period during the final two weeks of the season—Valentine was roasted for saying "If we don't make the playoffs I should be fired." For doing in effect the same thing Torre had done—taking the heat off his players—Valentine was called selfish for making himself the focal point.

By the way, in two of those losses, Ricky Henderson ran through a stop sign by third base coach Cookie Rojas and was out at the plate, while Shawon Dunston misplayed an 11th-inning long fly ball by the Braves' Brian Hunter that cost the Mets the game. On both occasions, when asked about the plays after the game, Valentine said he couldn't fault a player for being aggressive. Obviously, this was a cover-up answer—but what was he supposed to say? That Ricky made a bonehead play and Dunston should have caught the ball? No way: No smart big league manager is going to publicly criticize his players—he'll do it in private, but not in public. If he did, no one would want to play for him.

Speaking of the Mets, on the final Friday of the regular season, when they trailed both the Astros and the Reds by 2 games with only 3 to play, Channel 2 in New York sent me to Shea Stadium to do a live interview with Valentine for our 6:00 P.M. broadcast, just before a game with the Pirates. I asked myself all day long how I could approach Valentine to get him up for the interview. What angle could I take that hadn't been already used? The situation looked hopeless for the Mets: Just to force a 1-game playoff, either the Astros or Reds would have to lose 2 out of 3 while the Mets would need to win all 3 from the Pirates. Then it hit me: Look at the *bright* side! Don't hit the negative! I was ready for Valentine. Camera goes on, and I say, "Bobby, who are you going to start Monday in the 1-game playoff?" Well, he lit up. "Hey, that's the first positive thing I heard all week," he said. "I could start Yoshii." Next question: "Could you ever imagine at the start of the season that you could wind up possibly winning 96 games and still not be assured of making the playoffs?" He answered, "I'll take 96 wins any year and take my chances."

The Mets did win all 3 from the Pirates, and the Reds lost 2 of their 3 remaining games, forcing the single-game playoff in Cincinnati. (Valentine chose as his starter Al Leiter, not Masato Yoshii, who pitched a 2-hit shutout.)

"No Margin for Error"

In Game 1 of the 1999 playoff series between the Mets and the Diamondbacks, with the score tied 4–4 in the top of the 9th, bases loaded and one out for the Mets, Arizona manager Buck Showalter—who'd been relieved as manager of the Yankees after the 1995 season—brought in rookie reliever Bobby Chouinard to face Ricky Henderson and Edgardo Alfonzo. Chouinard got Henderson to ground out on a force play at home, but Alfonzo (known as The Fonz) hit a 3-1 pitch for a game-winning grand slam home run. Why did Buck go with Chouinard, who had been up and down in the minors three times during the season, while Matt Mantei, the Diamondbacks' number one closer with 22 saves out of 25 opportunities, sat in the bullpen?

After the game Showalter said, "There was no margin for error for Mantei." Yet in Game 4, the score tied 3–3 and the Mets threatening in the bottom of the 8th, Showalter left Mantei on the mound with the bases loaded and two outs. It was the same "no margin for error" situation. This time Mantei struck out Rey Ordonez to end the inning. He also pitched a scoreless 9th—before giving up Todd Pratt's game-winning homer in the 10th.

All I could think of is that if Bobby Valentine had done the same thing and brought in a rookie reliever rather than his number one right-handed closer, Armando Benitez, he would have been roasted unmercifully in the New York media. And to give it that lame excuse—"There was no margin for error for Mantei because the bases were loaded"—you gotta be kidding! That's what a closer is all about. That's his job when the game is on the line. And yet the Arizona press made no big deal about it. It was like San Diego the year before: The fans and the press were just happy to be in the playoffs, and it was all a great year.

By the way, just for the record, if you didn't want to start Randy Johnson in Game 4—though you're trailing in the series 2 games to 1—what about bringing him in in the 8th inning to preserve a 3–2 lead? All he has to do is get 6 outs, and you go back to Arizona the next day for the fifth and final game. Sure, you probably lose him for the fifth game—but if you don't win Game 4 (which they didn't) there is no Game 5.

Some Like It Hot

The temperature for Game 1 of the playoffs at Yankee Stadium last year dropped to 45 degrees. I asked Yogi Berra whether the cold was ever a problem for him. "Not for a catcher," Yogi replied. "We're always moving every pitch, plus you have the extra equipment—chest protector and a mask. The guys I always felt sorry for were the outfielders. [Yogi played a little outfield in his day.] It was cold, windy and lonely out there—and for the most part you had to stay in the same place, holding your position. For the infielders it wasn't as bad—they could shift around more than the outfielders. But for the catcher on a cold night—that was the place to be."

For pitchers, of course, it's strictly an individual call. Some, like Pedro Martinez, prefer the heat in order to stay loose. Some love the cold, which keeps them fresh, less chance of tiring.

Boston Red Sox = Misery

Just as I was preparing to leave for the ballpark for Game 1 of the Yankees–Red Sox ALCS, a fax comes in to the station. The letterhead says "Stephen King, Bangor, ME." Well, you'll recall King, the great mystery writer, had been hit by a truck six months before and had been hospitalized and was recuperating.

The fax says: "I watch you on Channel 2 from my satellite dish in western Maine. It's always CBS for me because I need a little 'Let's go to the videotape' in my day." But King goes on to say that I owe him and all the other Red Sox fans an apology, because when the team was losing Game 2 against Cleveland in the first round of the playoffs to go down 2 games to 0, I said Boston was dead.

So on the 6:00 P.M. news that night, which I did from Yankee Stadium, after explaining the letter to my audience, I say: "Mr. King, you are absolutely correct: I do owe you and all the Red Sox fans an apology. I was absolutely wrong. However, you know that book you wrote, *Misery*? If Pedro Martinez doesn't beat the Yanks in Game 3 you'll really know what misery is."

Running Out of Gas?

I got the chance to speak with Hall of Fame outfielder Enos "Country" Slaughter, who played nineteen years in the majors—most of them with the Cardinals—till he was forty-three. When asked the most he ever made, Slaughter—who finished with a lifetime batting average of .300 on the nose—said his top salary was $25,000 from the '49 Cards, who finished a game behind the Dodgers, who went on to play the Yankees in the Series that year (and lost, 4 games to 1). He added that when the season ended, the St. Louis newspapers said, "The Cardinals lost the pennant because Slaughter and his $25,000 salary ran out of gas."

Ran out of gas? All Slaughter did was hit .336, lead the league in triples and knock in 96 runs. "I hit .336!" he pointed out. "Today a guy hits .236 and he's a superstar."

Slaughter also talked about his famous "mad dash" from first on Harry Walker's double in the last of the 8th that won the decisive Game 7 of the 1946 World Series against the Red Sox.

According to Slaughter, in Game 1—lost by the Cards 3–2 in 10 innings—he hit a 2-out triple and would have scored on a bad relay but was held up at third by third base coach Mike Gonzalez. "After the game," Slaughter said, "Card manager Eddie Dyer told me to try and score on anything with two outs, regardless of whether Gonzalez tries to hold me up. Therefore, on Walker's hit in Game 7, I knew I was going to try and score as soon as I rounded second on the ball hit to left-center. I don't know if Gonzalez tried to hold me up, but I did expect Partee [Red Sox catcher Roy Partee] to try and block the plate, and I was ready to take him on."

To this day, Boston shortstop Johnny Pesky is accused of holding the relay too long and allowing Slaughter to score, but baseball historians will tell you that Pesky, who had his back to the plate to receive the throw, didn't realize until too late that Slaughter was still running and trying to score: He couldn't hear the shouts of his teammates above the roar of the crowd in tiny Sportsman Park.

And Just for the Record . . .

Just before Texas took the field for Game 2 of the first-round playoffs, Texas manager Bucky Dent said that if it were up to him, his team would not be playing the Yankees. He would have the wild card Red Sox playing the Yanks, while Texas, with the league's third best record, would face the Indians, who had the second best record. I agree 100 percent. It shouldn't matter that just because the Red Sox are in the same division as the Yankees they can't meet in the first round of the playoffs. One plays four and two plays three, period.

By the way, Dent, a former Yankee shortstop, is still remembered for the 3-run homer he hit off Mike Torrez in the 8th inning of that one-game playoff against the Red Sox in 1978. He had fouled an earlier pitch off his foot and called time-out. As he winced in pain, Mickey Rivers, sitting in the Yankee dugout, noticed that Dent was using a cracked bat. Dent said, "Rivers called over to me and said, 'Hey homey, you're using a broken bat.' " Rivers then gave Dent his bat, which he used to hit the home run.

After I had thanked Dent for the interview, he said, "And Warner, don't forget to tell the people I was not using a corked bat on the home run."

Keep on Moving

There were two bad calls at second base during the Red Sox–Yankees ALCS. In Game 1 Rick Reed ruled that Chuck Knoblauch held the ball long enough at second base for a force out on Jose Offerman—even though Knoblauch clearly dropped the ball. And in Game 4 Tim Tschida called Offerman out after a phantom tag by Knoblauch. (Both umpires admitted, after watching videotape, that they'd blown the calls.)

Joe Torre was later asked whether he favored videotape replay in baseball. "The problem I have with instant replay for baseball is this," he said. "Suppose the third base umpire misses a call, is challenged, and the videotape replay shows he was wrong and the call is reversed. Unlike football—where the official gets to move around the field after a call—the third base umpire has to stay in the same spot the rest of the game. The abuse from the fans could be awful for that third base umpire—he could become too much of a target."

He's right. Even in hockey, which uses videotape replay, the official is not only constantly moving, but he is protected by Plexiglas. It's an angle I never thought of until Torre brought it up.

The Class of Joe Torre

The night of what would be the final game of the World Series, I was on the field at Yankee Stadium for a live spot at 6:25. My whole angle was that I had two stories here: the fourth game of the season, and Roger Clemens. For Clemens, he was looking at a must win, or at least a strong performance—otherwise he could be booed out of town. A win and he looks good—he's off the hook. All is forgiven—even the 13–1 loss to Pedro Martinez and the Red Sox eleven days before. True there was no real pressure on Clemens to win Game 4, as far as the Series went. The Yanks were going to win: 4 games to 1, to 2, to 3, or to none. The Series was over, regardless what Clemens did that night. But the pressure was on Clemens to do well.

As my 6:25 spot approached, there was Torre behind the Yankees' batting cage. He's doing a taped interview with ESPN. The interview seems to go on forever. At 6:15 the Yankee PR man, doing his job, comes out and says, "Joe can't do anything after this. The ESPN interview was arranged weeks ago."

With that, Torre, who sees me waiting, ends the interview with ESPN and says, "Wait a minute, I just have to do one quick question with Warner." Now, in the same situation a lot of managers could have said That's it—I'm preparing for a ball game. But Torre did me a big favor and let us do the sound bite—and it was great. It filled in the missing hole in the broadcast. Not only did Torre answer my questions, but he captured the overall picture for me. I said, "Joe, this is it for Roger Clemens. He said he wanted a ring and it's laying out there on the mound for him to take." Torre, instead of downplaying the Clemens angle, said, "The stage is set, isn't it? I thought the Clemens-Martinez matchup was the high point, but this is it. When Roger joined us in spring training, he told me the most important thing to him was winning a World Series ring. That's why he signed with the Yanks."

Well, Clemens pitched 7⅔ innings, giving up only 4 hits, and left with a 3–0 lead. The Yankees went on to win the game 4–1, which clinched the Series 4–0.

I played the Torre interview back to the station with a few minutes to spare, and it made the evening news—thanks to Torre. He really is a nice guy who deserves all the success he has received.

Move the Fences Back!

Two questionable moves by Braves manager Bobby Cox— in the 8th inning of Game 1 and the 8th inning of Game 3— took him out of the 1999 World Series. In Game 1, with the score tied 1–1 and the Yankees batting in the top of the 8th, bases loaded and nobody out, Cox brings the infield in— inviting an easy 2-run single. Just like Padres manager Bruce Bochy in Game 4 of the '98 Series. What happens? Paul O'Neill hits a groundball that would have been a double play with the infield playing at normal depth but that goes into the hole between first and second and into right field. Two runs score, the Yankees add another run in the inning and they win 4–1. Now, true, a run would have scored on a double play, but the chances are at least even that you would have gotten out of the inning with just that one run, instead of still having two on, no outs and two runs in. Trailing 2–1 going into the bottom of the 8th is a lot different from trailing 4–1.

I said was: "Arizona against Valparaiso. If you had Valpo and 38 points . . . YOU LOST!!!"

And people loved it. Immediately. Imus, Bernard, Lou, Charles McCord, they kept shouting, "YOU LOST!" when I'd give them the setup.

Amazing. I think the gag works for a couple of reasons. First, people bet on these games and for the ones that do, the spread is more important than the score. Second, who would ever give or receive 38 points? The whole concept is so ridiculous that you laugh at the thought of anyone betting the game that way. And if *you* did . . . YOU LOST!

The next year, Kentucky clobbered UNC-Asheville 105–51. Think about that. If you had UNC-Asheville and 53 points, YOU LOST—and you were getting more points than UNC-Asheville even scored!

So that has become another trademark for me. I've heard it used in other walks of life—like describing the outcome of elections. It is probably my second biggest catchphrase, behind Let's go to the videotape. And it came out of nowhere.

So I'm going to use it right here.

If you thought this book would have one more chapter . . . YOU LOST!

And if you thought there were seven more letters to this book . . . YOU LOST!

T-H-E E-N-D.